THE MIELE
COOK BOOK

© Miele Company Limited

First published 1996

Reprinted 1997, 1999, 2000, 2002

Fifth reprint 2003

Special thanks to the Home Economics team at Miele Abingdon
who developed and tested all the recipes and methods used

The Miele Cook Book would like to acknowledge the help
of the following in the production of this book:

Design: Ted Skilbeck

Produced by: John Haycock

Photographs: Anthony Blake Photo Library

Colour reproduction: Keene Repro, London

Printed by: St Ives Roche, Cornwall

Bound by: MPG Books Ltd, Bodmin, Cornwall

ISBN 09509960 1 7

CONTENTS

Welcome to your new Miele oven which has been designed to give you a variety of oven functions coupled with superb technology. The recipes selected for this book by our team of Home Economists combine traditional dishes with exciting, new ideas to tempt and inspire you. All the recipes have been tested in the Miele ovens, and we hope they will help you to develop your own ideas and adapt your favourite recipes to your new oven.

The preparation times given for each recipe relate to the approximate length of time needed to prepare the ingredients only. Method times are not given as this will vary according to the capabilities of the cook.

Gas Mark	1	2	3	4	5	6	7	8	9
°F	275	300	325	350	375	400	425	450	475
°C	140	150	170	180	190	200	220	230	240

If some of your favourite recipes are in other cookery books, use this chart to find the approximate temperature.

Both metric and imperial measures are given in this book. Please use either all metric or all imperial measures. Do not mix them up, as they are not exact equivalents or conversions.

If preheating is recommended, select the temperature and the oven function, and preheat the oven for approximately 15 minutes.

THE OVEN FUNCTIONS

FAN HEAT The fan constantly circulates heat around the oven, giving a very even temperature throughout. This makes it possible to batch bake using several shelf positions and in many cases eliminates the need to preheat the oven. Unless the recipe states otherwise, place the food into a cold oven on the first shelf position. (Preheating may only be necessary for foods such as puff pastry and yeast mixtures, where instant heat is required to make them rise

quickly). The efficiency of this function means that temperatures for conventional recipes can be reduced by around 20°C and cooking times may also be slightly shorter. However, when you are batch baking and have a full oven, the cooking time should be extended slightly. See the diagram overleaf for advice on the best shelf positions to use for batch baking.

AUTO ROAST This function automatically seals and sears the meat and poultry at a high temperature (230°C), before returning to the pre-selected temperature to continue roasting.

TOP HEAT This is used for finishing gratins, browning, and cooking meringue toppings. This function is also useful for reheating food, ensuring that the centre of the food heats at the same rate as the topping crisps, e.g. Galway lamb bake and lasagne.

CONVENTIONAL With the conventional method of heating, radiant heat is directed onto the food from above and below. This function is particularly good for rich fruit cakes, pastries and breads, where a fairly long cooking time is required and a deep colour and good rise are needed. It is usually necessary to preheat the oven for about 20 minutes when using this method. The wire rack should always be used to allow the heat to circulate, placed in shelf position 2 or 3.

BOTTOM HEAT Ideal for reheating food with a pastry or dough base that needs to remain crisp.

DEFROST At this setting, air at room temperature is circulated to speed up the defrosting process.

INTENSIVE BAKE Intensive bake combines fan heat with a higher heat output from the floor element and a lower heat output from the roof element, making it ideal for foods which need a crisp base and a moist topping. It eliminates the need to blind bake most tarts, quiches and pizzas. Simply place the filling into the uncooked pastry case or spread onto the dough base. The first shelf position should always be used with this function, to take advantage of the bottom heat.

FAN GRILL The fan distributes the heat from the grill evenly over the food. Temperatures of up to 40°C lower can be used than would be selected for conventional grilling. This method is ideal for grilling thicker items such as stuffed meat, kebabs and pieces of poultry. The roasting filter should be in place to protect the fan from fat splashes, and the door should be kept closed, thus saving energy and minimizing cooking smells.

GRILL The grill is used for cooking flat items such as steaks, cutlets, fish and toasted snacks. It is divided into two zones, allowing you to use the full area (Grill 2) or the economy grill (Grill 1). Preheat the grill for 3–5 minutes before use. As with the fan grill, the door should remain closed with the roasting filter positioned over the fan.

ROASTING Traditionally, conventional heat is used for roasting, and a higher temperature is selected to seal the meat, then manually reduced to continue cooking. However, Miele recommends Auto roast, which is specially designed to give a crisp, succulent roast. Simply set up the deep roasting tray (see oven accessories) and put the meat on the wire rack. Place into the cold oven and select the desired roasting temperature. The oven automatically heats up to 230°C to seal the meat, retaining the juices and minimizing shrinkage, before reducing to the pre-selected temperature.

As a general rule, the larger the roast, the lower the temperature should be. Roasting will take longer at a lower temperature, but the result will be more even. For cuts over 3.2kg (7 lb), select a temperature 10°C lower than the standard suggestion. The roasting times given in these recipes allow for a slightly rare result (except for pork). If well-roasted meat is preferred, allow an extra 15–20 minutes' cooking time.

ROAST PROBE The roast probe gives a very accurate roasting result. It is inserted into the centre of a joint, where it constantly measures the internal temperature and automatically switches off the oven when the pre-selected temperature is reached. This ensures that roasting results can be repeated according to personal taste.

The probe should be inserted into the thickest part of the meat at an angle of 45°. It should not touch any bone or gristle, as these heat up more quickly than meat and may cause the probe to register the selected temperature too early. Place the meat on the deep roasting tray set up (see oven accessories) on the first shelf position, and plug the probe into the socket inside the oven. Once connected, select the oven function, then programme in your preferred temperature.

To test if the meat is cooked, (whether using the probe or the timed method), insert a sharp knife into the thickest part of the joint. If the juices run clear, the meat is ready. If the joint is not sufficiently cooked when the pre-selected temperature is reached, insert the probe into a different place and continue cooking.

Please note that the roast probe is not suitable for use with poultry, as there are too many bones for the probe to function properly.

OVEN ACCESSORIES

BAKING TRAYS The baking trays should be placed in the oven with the sloping edge towards the door. This ensures that heat can circulate evenly around the cavity. The trays are suitable for use with fan heat, intensive bake, top heat and bottom heat. Scones, vol-au-vents and biscuits, for example, can be placed directly on the trays, as can breads, baking tins and casserole dishes. When batch baking, the following shelf positions should be used, according to the number of trays being placed in the oven: 1 tray: 1st runner from bottom; 2 trays: 1st and 3rd runners from bottom; 3 trays: 1st, 2nd and 4th runners from bottom.

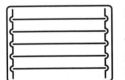

Fifth shelf
Fourth shelf
Third shelf
Second shelf
First shelf

WIRE RACK The wire rack is used in conjunction with conventional heating, where the heat needs to circulate freely through the oven.

SETTING UP FOR ROASTING AND GRILLING When roasting or grilling, use the deep sided tray. The anti-splash tray should be placed inside, and the wire rack locked into position around the edge of the roasting tray. This combination will slide into one shelf position.

ROASTING FILTER When roasting or grilling, the roasting filter should be placed over the fan to ensure that fat does not splash onto the blades. The filter must be removed when using fan heat, intensive bake and conventional settings, as it will impede the air flow around the cavity, giving uneven cooking results. Remember to remove and wash the filter after use.

ROAST PROBE Using the roast probe enables the roasting process to be monitored simply and reliably. Use of the Auto roast setting is recommended with this feature.

KEEPING YOUR OVEN CLEAN To ensure that your Miele oven remains in pristine condition, it is important that it is cleaned regularly and correctly, especially after roasting and grilling, when fat is distributed around the oven during cooking.

The sides, rear and roof of the oven have catalytic linings which oxidize fat, helping to keep the oven free of grease. The oven floor and door are coated with an extremely resistant form of enamel called Clean Enamel. A wipe with a cloth and mild, non-abrasive detergent should suffice to keep this clean. The door can be removed for easier access.

To clean the oven, first remove the accessories and shelf supports. Clean these with a non-abrasive cleaner. The oven floor and door should also be cleaned with a non-abrasive cleaner.

To clean the catalytic linings, switch the oven on to the highest possible temperature using the fan heat or conventional setting. Leave the oven on for approximately 1 hour, depending on the amount of soiling. If one cleaning process is insufficient, the procedure can be repeated a number of times until the liners are clean.

To clean very stubborn stains, remove the liners and wash the specific area with warm water, mild detergent and a pot brush, using gentle brush strokes. Rinse the liners carefully, replace in the oven and repeat the 1 hour cleaning process.

The front of the oven should be wiped with a soft cloth.

Keeping your oven clean will prevent stale cooking smells building up and will prolong the life of the catalytic liners.

If you require further advice on the use of your oven, we at Miele will be delighted to help you. Please write to us at: Miele Company Ltd, Fairacres, Marcham Rd, Abingdon, Oxon OX14 1TW.

CHICKEN & VEGETABLE TERRINE

STARTERS &
LIGHT DISHES

CREAM OF WATERCRESS SOUP

Preparation time:	Serves:	Total cooking time:
20 minutes	4–6	45 minutes

50g (2 oz) butter

350g (12 oz) leeks, white parts only, chopped

110g (4 oz) shallots, roughly chopped

2 medium potatoes, peeled and chopped

2 bunches, approx 150g (5 oz) watercress, chopped

Salt and freshly ground black pepper

850ml (1½ pints) chicken stock

150ml (5 fl oz) double cream

Single cream to garnish (optional)

Melt the butter in a heavy-based saucepan. Add the leeks, shallots, potatoes and watercress, and sauté for 2 minutes, stirring well. Season with salt and pepper. Cover with a tight-fitting lid and sweat the vegetables over a low heat for 20 minutes, shaking the pan occasionally. Add the stock and bring to the boil. Reduce the heat and simmer, covered, for about 10 minutes or until the vegetables are tender. Remove from the heat. Coarsely blend the soup and return to the saucepan. Stir in the cream and reheat, being careful not to boil. Garnish with a swirl of single cream before serving.

SMOKY BACON & VEGETABLE BROTH

Preparation time:	Serves:	Total cooking time:
30 minutes	4–6	1 hour 25 minutes

5ml (1 tsp) oil

8 rashers smoked streaky bacon, chopped

1 carrot, chopped

1 onion, chopped

1 stick of celery, finely chopped

150g (5 oz) red lentils

175g (6 oz) fresh tomatoes, chopped

2 cloves garlic, crushed

1.2 litres (2 pints) vegetable stock

175g (6 oz) cabbage, finely shredded

15ml (1 tbsp) chopped parsley

Salt and freshly ground black pepper

30ml (2 tbsp) double cream

Heat the oil in a large saucepan and fry the bacon for a few minutes. Add the carrot, onion and celery and stir over a fairly high heat for 10 minutes. Add the lentils, tomatoes and garlic and stir in the stock. Bring to the boil, then cover and simmer gently for 45 minutes. Add the cabbage and cook for a further 15 minutes. Liquidize the soup, then stir in the parsley and seasoning. Just before serving, swirl in the double cream, and serve with granary bread.

CREAM OF MUSHROOM SOUP

Preparation time:	Serves:	Total cooking time:
10 minutes	4	1 hour

Half a small onion, chopped

110g (4 oz) oyster mushrooms

110g (4 oz) button mushrooms

570ml (1 pint) vegetable stock

25g (1 oz) butter

45ml (3 level tbsp) plain flour

15ml (1 tbsp) cornflour

425ml (3/4 pint) creamy milk

Salt and freshly ground black pepper

45ml (3 tbsp) single cream

30ml (2 tbsp) fresh parsley, chopped

Place the onion and mushrooms in a saucepan with the vegetable stock. Bring to the boil, cover and simmer for 30 minutes. Melt the butter in a separate saucepan and add the flours. Cook for 2 minutes, then whisk in the milk and cook until the sauce thickens. Liquidize the mushrooms and stock until smooth. Stir into the white sauce. Season to taste and simmer for 15 minutes. Allow to cool slightly before stirring in the cream, then serve immediately garnished with parsley.

ROASTED TOMATO & RED PEPPER SOUP

Preparation time:	Serves:	Total cooking time:
10 minutes	4	45 minutes

1 red pepper, halved and deseeded

900g (2 lb) plum tomatoes, halved

50g (2 oz) butter and 2 sticks celery, finely chopped

1 onion, finely chopped and 1 clove garlic, crushed

275ml (1/2 pint) carton concentrated fresh chicken stock

30ml (2 tbsp) tomato purée

Salt and freshly ground black pepper

5ml (1 tsp) sugar, or to taste

30ml (2 tbsp) fresh basil leaves and celery to garnish

Place the pepper halves skin side up on the roasting tray and cook on Auto roast for 25 minutes. Scoop out the seeds from the tomatoes into a sieve, and press any juices and pulp into a bowl. Discard the seeds. Ten minutes before the end of the roasting time, add the tomato halves, skin side uppermost, and roast along with the pepper. Remove from the oven and cool slightly before removing the skins from the peppers and tomatoes. Chop roughly and reserve. Melt the butter in a large saucepan and sauté the celery, onion and garlic until soft but not coloured. Add the pepper and tomato flesh, any reserved juices, stock and purée, and bring slowly to the boil. Pour the mixture into a liquidizer and process until smooth. Alternatively, pass through a fine sieve. Return to the saucepan and reheat. Season well with salt, freshly ground black pepper and sugar to taste. Pour into warmed bowls and serve garnished with chopped basil leaves and celery.

Function	Cooking time	Preheating	Shelf position
Auto roast 200ºC	25 minutes	No	First

ROASTED TOMATO & RED PEPPER SOUP

SMOKED HADDOCK CHOWDER

Preparation time:	Serves:	Total cooking time:
15 minutes	4–6	30 minutes

225g (8 oz) potatoes, peeled and diced

275ml (½ pint) whole milk

110ml (4 fl oz) single cream

200ml (7 fl oz) dry white wine

Good pinch of saffron threads

1 bayleaf

30ml (2 tbsp) olive oil

50g (2 oz) bacon, diced

1 onion, chopped

450g (1 lb) undyed smoked haddock, skinned

Salt and freshly ground black pepper

45ml (3 tbsp) fresh parsley, chopped

Place the potatoes in a saucepan with the milk, cream, wine, saffron and bayleaf. Bring to the boil, then reduce the heat and simmer until the potatoes are just cooked but still firm. Meanwhile, heat the oil in a frying pan and sauté the bacon until it starts to brown. Add the onion and fry until softened, without browning. Transfer to the saucepan with the potatoes. Cut the fish into chunks and add to the other ingredients. Simmer until the fish is just cooked. Season with plenty of freshly ground black pepper, and salt if necessary. Sprinkle on the fresh parsley, and serve immediately.

GRILLED STUFFED FIELD MUSHROOMS

Preparation time:	Serves:	Total cooking time:
10 minutes	4	12–15 minutes

4 large field mushrooms

125g (4½ oz) cream cheese with garlic and herbs

2 drops of Tabasco sauce

Salt and freshly ground black pepper

60g (2½ oz) dried breadcrumbs

5ml (1 tsp) fresh parsley

5ml (1 tsp) garlic purée

30ml (2 tbsp) olive oil

150ml (5 fl oz) vegetable stock

Peel the mushrooms, if dirty, and trim the stalks. Beat the cream cheese and Tabasco sauce together and spread over the mushrooms, completely covering the gills. Sprinkle with a little salt and freshly ground black pepper. In a bowl, mix together the breadcrumbs and parsley. In a separate bowl, blend the garlic purée and olive oil. Mix into the breadcrumbs, stirring well until they are coated in garlic oil. Divide the mixture evenly between the cream cheese-filled mushrooms, completely covering the cheese. Place in a shallow ovenproof dish, and pour the vegetable stock around the mushrooms. Grill until the breadcrumbs are a deep golden brown colour and the mushrooms are cooked. Serve immediately.

Function	Cooking time	Preheating	Shelf position
Fan grill 250ºC	12–15 minutes	Yes	Fourth

INDIVIDUAL BLUE CHEESE SOUFFLES

Preparation time:	Serves:	Total cooking time:
10 minutes + infusing	4	30 minutes

225ml (8 fl oz) milk

1 small onion, quartered

1 bayleaf

3 black peppercorns

Pinch of grated nutmeg

Pinch of salt

25g (1 oz) unsalted butter

25g (1 oz) self-raising flour

2 eggs, separated

10ml (2 tsp) chives, snipped

110g (4 oz) Danish Blue cheese, crumbled

Put the milk, onion, bayleaf, peppercorns, nutmeg and salt into a small saucepan. Slowly bring up to simmering point, then remove from the heat and leave to infuse for 15 minutes. Strain into a jug and discard the flavourings. Melt the butter in a clean saucepan and stir in the flour. Cook for 1–2 minutes, then gradually add the milk, whisking continuously until the sauce thickens. Remove from the heat and beat in the egg yolks and chives. Add the Danish blue cheese. Whisk the egg whites to soft peaks and lightly fold into the cheese mixture. Divide between 4 well buttered ramekins and bake for 20 minutes until well risen, golden and firm to the touch. The surface should be crispy with a soft set centre.

Function	Cooking time	Preheating	Shelf position
Fan heat 180°C	20 minutes	Yes	First

VEGETABLE PATE WITH WATERCRESS SAUCE

Preparation time:	Serves:	Total cooking time:
10 minutes	4–6	1 hour 10 minutes

350g (12 oz) cauliflower florets

350g (12 oz) carrots, thinly sliced

Salt and freshly ground black pepper

1 egg, beaten

150ml (5 fl oz) double cream

1.25ml (¼ tsp) freshly grated nutmeg

1.25ml (¼ tsp) ground coriander

Sauce 1 bunch of watercress, washed and trimmed

75ml (5 tbsp) fromage frais

15ml (1 tbsp) lemon juice

Pinch of salt

Boil the cauliflower and carrots in separate saucepans of salted water until just tender. Drain both vegetables well, then purée them separately until smooth. Transfer to separate bowls. Mix half the egg and cream into the cauliflower, and half into the carrots, seasoning well. Stir the nutmeg into the cauliflower, and the coriander into the carrots. Lightly butter a 450g (1 lb) loaf tin. Put half the cauliflower purée in the bottom, and spread evenly. Cover with a layer of carrot purée. Repeat, ending with a layer of carrot purée. Cover tightly with foil and bake in the oven for an hour, or until set. Leave to rest in the tin for 5 minutes before turning out. To make the sauce, place all the remaining ingredients in a blender and purée until smooth. Serve with slices of the pâté.

Function	Cooking time	Preheating	Shelf position
Fan heat 170°C	1 hour	No	First

WILD MUSHROOMS ON BRIOCHE
WITH HERB CREAM SAUCE

Preparation time:	Serves:	Total cooking time:
10 minutes	4	10 minutes

25g (1 oz) butter

1 shallot, finely chopped

1 clove garlic, crushed

200g (7 oz) wild mushrooms, cleaned

5ml (1 tsp) lemon juice

Salt and freshly ground black pepper

150ml (5 fl oz) soured cream

5ml (1 tsp) fresh chervil, chopped

5ml (1 tsp) fresh parsley, chopped

4 thick slices of brioche

Fresh herbs to garnish

Melt the butter in a saucepan and sauté the shallot and garlic until soft and translucent. Slice the mushrooms, and add to the pan along with the lemon juice and seasoning. Cover with a lid and cook over a medium heat for 2 minutes. Stir in the soured cream and herbs, then cover and cook for a further 2 minutes. Toast the slices of brioche under a preheated grill until golden brown on each side (watch carefully because they colour very quickly). Spoon the mushrooms and sauce onto the brioche, garnish with herbs and serve immediately.

Function	Cooking time	Preheating	Shelf position
Grill 300ºC	25–30 seconds	Yes	Fifth

CRISPY POTATO SKINS
WITH SOUR CREAM DIP

Preparation time:	Serves:	Total cooking time:
5 minutes	4	1 hour 25 minutes

	4 large baking potatoes
	Oil to brush
Dip	25g (1 oz) torta dolcelatte cheese
	1 clove garlic, crushed
	15ml (1 tbsp) chives, chopped
	Black pepper
	150ml (5 fl oz) soured cream

Wash and pierce the skin of each potato with a fork. Place on a baking tray and cook on fan heat for about 1 hour 15 minutes until the potatoes are cooked through. Cool slightly, then cut into quarters lengthways and scoop out the potato, leaving a thin layer next to the skin. Brush the skins all over with oil and place them on the wire rack. Cook under the preheated grill until the skins are crisp and brown. Meanwhile, to make the dip, beat all the remaining ingredients together until smooth and creamy. Serve with the crispy skins.

Baking potatoes

Function	Cooking time	Preheating	Shelf position
Fan heat 190ºC	1 hr 15 mins	No	First

Crisping skins

Function	Cooking time	Preheating	Shelf position
Fan grill 230ºC	10 minutes	Yes	Fourth

SALMON & PEPPERED CHEESE PARCELS

Preparation time:	Makes:	Total cooking time:
10 minutes	24 approximately	15 minutes

225g (8 oz) salmon fillet, skinned

Freshly grated nutmeg

150g (5 oz) peppered cream cheese

30ml (2 tbsp) grated lemon rind

Salt and freshly ground black pepper

150g (5 oz) filo pastry

50g (2 oz) melted butter

Sesame seeds

Finely chop the salmon fillet, then mix with the nutmeg, peppered cream cheese, lemon rind, salt and pepper. To form the parcels, take a sheet of filo pastry and cut in half lengthways. Brush with melted butter. Place a generous teaspoon of the mixture at one end of the pastry, then fold repeatedly to form a triangle shape. Brush with melted butter and sprinkle with sesame seeds. Place on a lightly greased baking tray and bake until crisp and golden brown.

Function	Cooking time	Preheating	Shelf position
Fan heat 190ºC	15 minutes	Yes	First

CARAMELIZED THAI FISH

Preparation time:	Serves:	Total cooking time:
5 minutes + marinading	4	4–6 minutes

4 small plaice fillets

5ml (1 tsp) salt

Juice 1 lime

2 spring onions, finely shredded

60ml (4 tbsp) soft light brown sugar

Shredded spring onions to garnish

Remove the skin from the fillets, then halve each one lengthways. Sprinkle with the salt and lime juice. Divide the spring onions between the fillets, laying them in the centre, then roll up the fish. Place in the refrigerator to marinate for 30 minutes. Coat the surface of the rolled-up fish in sugar, and place on a baking tray. Cook under the preheated grill for 4–6 minutes, depending on size, until cooked. Turn the fillets halfway through the cooking time. Serve immediately, garnished with shredded spring onions.

Function	Cooking time	Preheating	Shelf position
Grill 240ºC	4 – 6 minutes	Yes	Third/Fourth

SALMON MOUSSE

Preparation time:	Serves:	Total cooking time:
15 minutes + chilling	6	35 minutes

25g (1 oz) butter and 2 spring onions, finely chopped

25g (1 oz) plain flour and 200ml (7 fl oz) milk

Good pinch of paprika

Salt and freshly ground black pepper

350g (12 oz) fresh salmon, skinned and boned

5ml (1 tsp) finely grated lemon rind

15ml (1 tbsp) lemon juice

30ml (2 tbsp) fresh parsley, chopped

1 egg, beaten and 25g (1 oz) butter, melted

Thin cucumber slices

Grease 6 individual ramekin dishes. Melt the butter in a saucepan and sauté the spring onions until soft. Stir in the flour and cook for 1–2 minutes. Gradually whisk in the milk and bring to the boil, stirring continuously. Reduce the heat and cook for 2–3 minutes, stirring, until the sauce has thickened. Add the paprika and season to taste. Process the salmon until smooth. Mix the fish, lemon rind, juice, parsley and egg thoroughly into the sauce. Divide the mixture between the ramekin dishes and spoon over half the melted butter. Place the dishes in the deep roasting tray or suitable dish and add enough hot water to come halfway up the sides of the ramekins. Bake in the oven until the mousse is just firm to the touch. Spoon the remaining melted butter evenly over the mousse, and leave to chill for at least 1 hour. Garnish with thin slices of cucumber and serve with Melba toast.

Function	Cooking time	Preheating	Shelf position
Fan heat 150°C	20 – 25 minutes	No	First

SMOKED HADDOCK & DILL PARCELS

Preparation time:	Serves:	Total cooking time:
10 minutes	4	40 minutes

50g (2 oz) butter

3 shallots, finely chopped

350g (12 oz) smoked haddock, skinned, boned & chopped

150ml (¼ pint) dry white wine

3 peppercorns and some fresh dill, chopped

5ml (1 tsp) plain flour

30ml (2 tbsp) single cream

8 sheets filo pastry

Melt half the butter in a saucepan and gently fry the shallots until translucent. Add the haddock and cook gently until opaque. Add half the wine and heat until the fish is just cooked. Remove the haddock with a slotted spoon, flake and put to one side. Add the remaining wine, peppercorns and dill to the saucepan. Bring to the boil, reduce the heat and simmer until the liquid has reduced by half. Mix half of the remaining butter and the flour to a paste, and whisk into the sauce to thicken. Add the cream and the flaked fish, then leave to cool. Cut the pastry sheets in half to make squares. Melt the remaining butter and brush the pastry sheets, layering up in fours, offsetting each sheet to create a star shape. Divide the fish mixture between the pastry, piling into the centre. Bring the corners of the pastry up to meet over the fish, and squeeze together. Twist the top to form a sack, and open out the corners to give a frill. Brush with the remaining butter and bake until the pastry is crisp and golden.

Function	Cooking time	Preheating	Shelf position
Fan heat 190°C	15 – 20 minutes	Yes	First

SMOKED HADDOCK & DILL PARCELS

DUBLIN BAY PRAWNS WITH PARMA HAM

Preparation time:	Serves:	Total cooking time:
15 minutes + marinading	4	5 minutes

60g (2¹/₂ oz) sliced Parma ham

200g (7 oz) Dublin Bay prawns, cooked and shelled

1 lemon

1 shallot, finely chopped

1 clove garlic, crushed

5ml (1 tsp) wholegrain mustard

1 fresh red chilli, seeded

60ml (4 tbsp) olive oil

Salt and freshly ground black pepper

Have ready eight small metal or wooden skewers. Cut the Parma ham into strips and wrap it tightly around the prawns. Cut the lemon in half, and cut one half into eight wedges. Thread one lemon wedge onto each skewer. Extract the juice from the other half of the lemon and reserve for the marinade. Thread the wrapped prawns onto the skewers and place in a dish. Mix the remaining ingredients together and pour over the prawns. Cover and leave in the refrigerator to marinate for 2 hours, turning occasionally. Remove the prawns from the marinade, and grill on a wire rack over the deep roasting tray. Baste with marinade and turn occasionally until the prawns are heated through and the ham begins to crisp. Serve with salad-stuffed pitta breads or on a bed of rice.

Function	Cooking time	Preheating	Shelf position
Grill 200ºC	5 minutes	Yes	Fourth

GRILLED AVOCADO WITH PRAWNS

Preparation time:	Serves:	Total cooking time:
10 minutes	4	10 minutes

125g (4¹/₂ oz) Bel Paese semi-hard cheese, chilled & grated

175g (6 oz) fresh peeled prawns

5ml (1 tsp) chives, chopped

Salt and freshly ground black pepper

2 large ripe avocados

15ml (1 tbsp) lemon juice

2 tomatoes, sliced

Pinch of cayenne pepper

Green salad leaves

Place 50g (2 oz) of Bel Paese in a bowl with the prawns and chives. Mix together and season. Cut the avocados in half lengthways. Remove the stone but do not peel. Brush with lemon juice to prevent discoloration. Cut a small slice off the rounded side of each so that they sit flat, and place on a baking tray. Divide the cheese and prawn mixture between the avocados. Arrange the tomato slices on top, and cover with the remaining Bel Paese. Season with cayenne pepper. Place under the preheated grill and cook until the cheese has browned and the avocado is warm. Serve with green salad leaves.

Function	Cooking time	Preheating	Shelf position
Grill 250ºC	10 minutes	Yes	Fourth

CHICKEN & VEGETABLE TERRINE

Preparation time:	Serves:	Total cooking time:
10 minutes	4–6	1 hour 30 – 45 mins

60g (2½ oz) fine green beans

1 medium carrot, cut into julienne strips

Half a fennel bulb, chopped

Half a red pepper, sliced

10 baby sweetcorns

4 Chinese leaves

275g (10 oz) cooked chicken

3 eggs

200g (7 oz) cream cheese

Salt and white pepper

10ml (2 tsp) tomato purée

Blanch the green beans, carrots, fennel, red pepper, sweetcorn and Chinese leaves separately in boiling water until just tender. Plunge immediately into cold water. Liquidize the chicken, eggs, cream cheese, seasoning and tomato purée together until smooth and creamy. Oil a 450g (1 lb) terrine or loaf tin. Line the base and sides of the tin with Chinese leaves, overlapping to ensure there are no gaps. Spoon a layer of the chicken purée into the tin and spread evenly. Follow with a layer of green beans, then another layer of chicken purée. Continue to layer the purée and vegetables, and finish with a layer of the chicken. Place the terrine in the deep roasting tray or suitable tin, half-filled with hot water, and cook in the oven until set. Leave to cool in the terrine, then turn out and serve in slices.

Function	Cooking time	Preheating	Shelf position
Conventional 170ºC	1 hr 15 – 30 mins	Yes	First

INDONESIAN PORK SATAY

Preparation time:	Serves:	Total cooking time:
10 minutes + marinading	4	35 minutes

350g (12 oz) pork fillet

30ml (2 tbsp) dark soy sauce

45ml (3 tbsp) lemon juice

7.5ml (1½ tsp) ground ginger

30ml (2 tbsp) vegetable oil

110g (4 oz) unsalted peanuts, chopped

1 clove garlic, crushed and 1.25ml (¼ tsp) salt

2.5ml (½ tsp) ground coriander

1.25ml (¼ tsp) chilli powder and 425ml (¾ pint) coconut milk

5ml (1 tsp) soft brown sugar

Half a small cucumber

Cut the pork fillet into small, even sized cubes. In a bowl mix together the soy sauce, lemon juice and 5ml (1 tsp) of the ginger. Add the pork to the bowl, mixing well to coat completely in the marinade. Leave to marinate for about 30 minutes, stirring occasionally. Meanwhile, heat the oil in a saucepan. Add the peanuts, garlic, salt, coriander, chilli powder and remaining ginger and fry for 4 minutes. Stir in the coconut milk and sugar, bring to the boil and simmer for 15 minutes or until the sauce has thickened. Thread the marinated pork onto 8 skewers. Season and fan grill on the wire rack for 8–10 minutes, turning occasionally until the meat is cooked. Slice the cucumber thinly and serve with the meat and the hot satay sauce.

Function	Cooking time	Preheating	Shelf position
Fan grill 200ºC	8 – 10 minutes	Yes	Fourth

CHICKEN LIVER PATE

SMOKED BACON & SPINACH TIMBALES

Preparation time:	Serves:	Total cooking time:
15 minutes	6	50 minutes

10g (½ oz) butter

3 shallots, finely chopped

1 rasher smoked bacon, chopped

225g (8 oz) chopped spinach

150ml (5 fl oz) single cream

2 eggs, beaten

50g (2 oz) mature Cheddar, grated

25g (1 oz) fresh wholemeal breadcrumbs

2.5ml (½ tsp) grated nutmeg

Salt and freshly ground black pepper

Cherry tomatoes to garnish

Melt the butter in a large saucepan and sauté the shallots and bacon until cooked. Add the spinach and cook for a further 2 minutes. Stir in the remaining ingredients. Spoon the mixture into 6 buttered ramekin dishes. Cover with foil and place in the deep roasting tray or suitable dish, half-filled with hot water. Bake until set. Turn out onto a warmed serving plate and garnish with cherry tomatoes, or serve with a tomato coulis (see page 140).

Function	Cooking time	Preheating	Shelf position
Fan heat 180ºC	40 minutes	No	First

CHICKEN LIVER PATE

Preparation time:	Serves:	Total cooking time:
10 minutes + chilling	4	15 minutes

110g (4 oz) butter

1 small onion, finely chopped

1 clove garlic, crushed

225g (8oz) chicken livers, chopped

45ml (3 tbsp) double cream

10ml (2 tsp) tomato purée

10ml (2 tsp) brandy

Salt and freshly ground black pepper

1 bayleaf and black peppercorns

Melt half the butter in a saucepan, and gently fry the onion and garlic for 5 minutes. Add the chicken livers and cook for a further 5 minutes. Leave to cool slightly, then stir in the cream, tomato purée, brandy and seasoning. Purée the mixture until smooth, then spoon into a serving dish. Melt the remaining butter and drizzle over the pâté. Place a bayleaf and a few peppercorns lightly on the surface, then leave to chill for at least 2 hours, or until set. Serve with Melba toast.

INDIAN SAMOSAS

Preparation time:	Makes:	Total cooking time:
30 minutes	24 approximately	55 minutes

15ml (1 tbsp) olive oil

225g (8 oz) lean minced beef

Half an onion, finely chopped

Half a red pepper, finely chopped

30ml (2 tbsp) tomato purée

225g (8 oz) fresh tomatoes, skinned, deseeded and chopped

5ml (1 tsp) Worcester sauce

10ml (2 tsp) garam masala

2.5ml (½ tsp) ground cumin

Pinch of paprika

2.5ml (½ tsp) ground cinnamon

150g (5 oz) filo pastry

50g (2 oz) melted butter

Poppy seeds

Heat the oil in a saucepan and fry the minced beef until brown. Stir in the onion and red pepper and cook until soft. Mix in the tomato purée, tomatoes, Worcester sauce and spices. Simmer gently uncovered for 30 minutes. Remove from the heat and cool. To form the samosas, fold a sheet of filo pastry lengthways in half and brush with melted butter on both sides. Place a generous teaspoon of the filling on the end of the pastry, and fold over repeatedly to form a triangle shape. Brush with butter and sprinkle with poppy seeds. Place on a lightly greased baking tray and bake until crisp and golden.

Function	Cooking time	Preheating	Shelf position
Fan heat 190ºC	15 minutes	No	First

ORANGE & HONEY BARBECUED RIBS

Preparation time:	Serves:	Total cooking time:
10 minutes + marinading	4	50 minutes

15ml (1 tbsp) lemon juice

15ml (1 tbsp) Worcester sauce

5ml (1 tsp) soy sauce

60ml (4 tbsp) clear honey

Juice and grated rind of 2 oranges

Salt and freshly ground black pepper

1.8kg (4 lb) pork spare ribs (approximately 8)

Sesame seeds to garnish

Place the lemon juice, Worcester sauce, soy sauce and honey in a saucepan. Add the juice and grated rind of the oranges and season. Heat gently to simmering point, stirring occasionally. Leave to cool, then pour over the meat. Leave the pork to marinate in the refrigerator for at least 3 hours, ideally overnight. Drain and reserve the marinade. Place the ribs in the deep roasting tray and cook on fan heat, basting occasionally. Then, to crisp the fat, place the cooked ribs under a preheated fan grill at 220ºC and cook for about 5 minutes on each side. Alternatively, transfer to a barbecue grill. Sprinkle with sesame seeds before serving with the marinade.

Function	Cooking time	Preheating	Shelf position
Fan heat 190ºC	40 minutes	No	First

Function	Cooking time	Preheating	Shelf position
Fan grill 220ºC	10 minutes	Yes	Fourth

ORANGE & HONEY BARBECUED RIBS

RILLETTES DE PORC

HOT & SPICY CHICKEN SALAD

Preparation time:	Serves:	Total cooking time:
15 minutes + marinading	4	8–10 minutes

2 large skinless chicken breast fillets

10ml (2 tsp) fresh root ginger, grated

Salt and freshly ground black pepper

45ml (3 tbsp) soy sauce

30ml (2 tbsp) vegetable oil

1 carrot, cut into julienne strips

40g (1½ oz) beansprouts

2 spring onions, sliced, including green parts

15ml (1 tbsp) sesame seed oil

15ml (1 tbsp) sesame seeds

15ml (1 tbsp) fresh red chilli, deseeded
or 2.5ml (½ tsp) dried crushed chillies

5ml (1 tsp) soft brown sugar

30ml (2 tbsp) dry sherry

Chinese leaves, shredded

Spring onions, shredded

Rub the chicken fillets all over in ginger, salt and pepper. Slice them into thick strips and put in a shallow dish. Pour over half the soy sauce and place in the refrigerator to marinate for 30 minutes. Heat 15ml (1 tbsp) of the vegetable oil in a saucepan. Add the chicken pieces and sauté for about 6 minutes or until cooked. Remove the chicken, cover, and leave to cool. Once cool, add the carrot, beansprouts and spring onions to the chicken. Heat the remaining vegetable oil and the sesame oil in a small saucepan. Add the sesame seeds and chilli and cook for 1 minute. Remove from the heat and cool slightly before stirring in the remaining soy sauce, sugar and sherry. Pour over the chicken and vegetables, cover and leave to marinate in the refrigerator for at least 1 hour, preferably overnight. Line a serving dish with shredded Chinese leaves. Arrange the chicken on top, pour over the marinade and garnish with shredded spring onions.

RILLETTES DE PORC

Preparation time:	Makes:	Total cooking time:
5 minutes + standing	1.25 kg (2½ lb)	3 hours 30 minutes

1.4kg (3 lb) belly pork

Salt

1 clove garlic, skinned and bruised

Bouquet garni

Freshly ground black pepper

Rind the belly pork, and bone if necessary. Sprinkle well with salt, ensuring that all the meat is coated. Leave to stand in a cool place for 4 hours. Cut the meat into thin strips, and place in an ovenproof dish. Bury the clove of garlic and bouquet garni in the centre and season with pepper. Add 75ml (3 fl oz) of water. Cover with a lid and cook for 3 hours 30 minutes. Discard the bouquet garni and garlic. Strain off the fat and reserve. Pound the meat and fat and pull into fine shreds. Pile into 2 x 275ml (½ pint) pâté dishes. Cover immediately with some of the reserved fat and chill until set. Serve at room temperature with crusty French bread and full-bodied red wine.

Function	Cooking time	Preheating	Shelf position
Fan heat 135ºC	3 hrs 30 mins	No	First

BAKED SALMON WITH GARLIC & DILL

FISH & SEAFOOD

BAKED SALMON
WITH GARLIC & DILL

Preparation time:	Serves:	Total cooking time:
5 minutes	4	15 – 20 minutes

4 x 150g (5 oz) salmon fillets

110g (4 oz) butter, softened

2 large cloves garlic, crushed

45ml (3 tbsp) fresh dill, chopped

15ml (1 tbsp) fresh parsley, chopped

5ml (1 tsp) lemon rind

5ml (1 tsp) lemon juice

Salt and freshly ground black pepper

5ml (1 tsp) olive oil

Place the salmon fillets in a single layer in an ovenproof baking dish. Blend together the butter, garlic, herbs, lemon rind and juice and season. Spread the herb butter evenly over the fillets. Cover the dish tightly with oiled silver foil, and bake until the fish is just cooked. Remove from the oven, cover and leave to stand for 5 minutes. Serve the fish with the melted herb butter and new potatoes.

Function	Cooking time	Preheating	Shelf position
Fan heat 200ºC	15–20 minutes	No	First

SALMON &
SAFFRON PIE

Preparation time:	Serves:	Total cooking time:
15 minutes	4	35 minutes

700g (1½ lb) salmon fillet, thick end

Salt and freshly ground black pepper

350g (12 oz) puff pastry

30ml (2 tbsp) couscous

1 large apple and the zest and juice of half a lemon

45ml (3 tbsp) fresh dill, chopped

50g (2 oz) butter, 3 eggs, good pinch of saffron threads

275ml (½ pint) single cream

Cut the fish into 4cm (1½ inch) cubes, and season with salt and pepper. Roll out ⅔ of the pastry on a floured surface, and use to line a pie dish. Sprinkle the couscous into the bottom. Slice the apple thinly, dip in lemon juice, and blot on kitchen paper. Arrange half the apple over the couscous. Place the salmon pieces on top, sprinkle with the lemon zest and dill. Top with the remaining apple slices and dot with butter. Roll out the remaining pastry and use to cover the pie, making sure the edges are well sealed. Whisk 1 egg with a little salt and use to glaze the pie. Cut a small hole in the top and insert a pastry funnel. Bake in the oven on the wire rack at 190ºC for 20 minutes. Meanwhile, infuse the saffron threads in 45ml (3 tbsp) of boiling water. Stir into the cream, then whisk in the remaining 2 eggs. Remove the pie from the oven and increase the heat to 200ºC. Pour the saffron custard into the pie via the funnel. Return to the oven and bake for a further 15 minutes until crisp and golden.

Function	Cooking time	Preheating	Shelf position
Conv. 190 + 200ºC	20 + 15 minutes	Yes	Second

DELUXE FISH PIE

Preparation time:	Serves:	Total cooking time:
20 minutes	4 – 6	40 minutes

450g (1 lb) potatoes, thinly sliced

Salt and freshly ground black pepper

75g (3 oz) butter

110g (4 oz) button mushrooms, wiped

225g (8 oz) peeled prawns

4 scallops, washed and sliced

450g (1 lb) cod, boned and cut into 2.5cm (1 inch) cubes

30ml (2 tbsp) parsley, finely chopped

60ml (4 tbsp) dry white wine

275g (10 oz) packet filo pastry

Boil the potatoes with a little salt and pepper until just cooked. Melt 25g (1 oz) of the butter, pour into a pie dish and arrange the potato slices in the bottom. Scatter over the mushrooms, prawns, scallops and cod. Add the parsley and wine. Season and dot with a further 25g (1oz) of butter. Melt the remaining butter and use to brush the individual filo pastry sheets. Arrange on top of the pie in puckered layers to give an attractive finish. Bake until the pastry is a rich golden colour, and serve hot with a selection of fresh green vegetables.

Function	Cooking time	Preheating	Shelf position
Fan heat 200°C	30 minutes	No	First

SPICY FISH CAKES

Preparation time:	Serves:	Total cooking time:
25 minutes	4 – 6	12 minutes

1 green medium hot chilli

4 spring onions, including green parts

700g (1½ lb) mashed potatoes

Salt and freshly ground black pepper

350g (12 oz) cooked fresh crab meat or any cooked white fish

60ml (4 tbsp) plain flour

2 eggs, beaten

110g (4 oz) fine breadcrumbs

Finely chop the chilli and the spring onions. Mix into the potato, and season well. Lightly stir in the crab meat. Divide the mixture and shape into 12 rounds. Arrange 3 plates in a row. Put the flour on the first, the egg on the second and the breadcrumbs on the third one. Dust the fish cakes lightly with flour, dip them in the egg, and finally coat them thoroughly with breadcrumbs. Arrange the fish cakes on a baking tray, and grill for about 6 minutes on each side or until golden brown. Serve with a tomato coulis (see page 140).

Function	Cooking time	Preheating	Shelf position
Fan grill 250°C	12 minutes	No	Fourth

SPICY FISH CAKES

BUTTERY KEDGEREE

BAKED HALIBUT
WITH GREEN HERB SAUCE

Preparation time:	Serves:	Total cooking time:
10 minutes	4	20 – 25 minutes

3 spring onions, sliced

8 fresh mint leaves

20g (3/4 oz) fresh coriander leaves

Few sprigs of parsley

3 sprigs lemon thyme

1 stalk lemon grass, thinly sliced

Piece of green chilli

1 clove garlic, peeled

Salt and freshly ground black pepper

Pinch of sugar

15ml (1 tbsp) lemon juice

45ml (3 tbsp) extra virgin olive oil

15 – 30 ml (1 – 2 tbsp) warm water

4 x 175g (6 oz) halibut or hake cutlets

Put the spring onions, mint, coriander leaves stripped from the stem, parsley and lemon thyme into a food processor. Add the lemon grass, green chilli, garlic, salt, pepper and sugar, and process finely. Blend in the lemon juice, 30ml (2 tbsp) of the oil and a little water to make a paste. Brush an ovenproof dish with the remaining olive oil and spoon a little of the green sauce into the base. Place the fish cutlets on top and spread the remaining sauce over the fish. Bake in the oven until the fish is cooked. Cover and leave to rest for 5 minutes, then serve with gratin dauphinois potatoes (see page 92).

Function	Cooking time	Preheating	Shelf position
Fan heat 185ºC	20 – 25 minutes	No	First

BUTTERY KEDGEREE

Preparation time:	Serves:	Total cooking time:
15 minutes	4	25 minutes

350g (12 oz) smoked haddock fillet, skinned

110g (4 oz) butter

1 onion, chopped

5ml (1 tsp) madras curry powder

200g (7 oz) quick-cook long grain rice

2 hard boiled eggs, sliced

45ml (3 tbsp) fresh parsley, chopped

15ml (1 tbsp) lemon juice

Freshly ground black pepper

Hard boiled egg and parsley to garnish

Cut the fish into pieces and place in a saucepan. Pour on 450ml (16 fl oz) of boiling water, bring back to the boil and simmer for 4 – 5 minutes, or until the fish is opaque and just cooked. Drain off the water into a measuring jug and reserve. Place the fish in a bowl, cover with clingfilm and keep warm. Melt half the butter in a saucepan and fry the onion until soft. Stir in the curry powder and cook for 30 seconds. Add the rice and stir to coat in the butter. Pour on the reserved fish cooking liquor, bring to the boil, then simmer for about 15 minutes until the rice is tender. Flake the fish and fold into the rice, together with the sliced eggs, parsley, lemon juice, remaining butter and freshly ground black pepper. Warm through over a gentle heat for 2 – 3 minutes. Garnish with slices of hardboiled egg and parsley.

PAELLA

PAELLA

Preparation time:	Serves:	Total cooking time:
20 minutes	4 – 6	40 minutes

15ml (1 tbsp) oil and 450g (1 lb) boneless chicken, cubed

1 onion, chopped and 2 cloves garlic, crushed

350g (12 oz) long grain rice

1.2 litres (2 pints) boiling chicken stock

5ml (1 tsp) paprika and 2.5ml (½ tsp) saffron powder

Salt and freshly ground black pepper

3 tomatoes, cut into wedges

1 large red pepper, sliced into thin strips

50g (2 oz) garden peas

150g (5 oz) mussels, drained

250g (9 oz) cooked prawns, peeled

110g (4 oz) whole cooked king prawns

Lemon wedges to garnish

Heat the oil in a large deep frying pan and sauté the chicken pieces until golden brown. Remove the chicken from the pan and reserve. Add the onion and garlic and fry gently for 5 minutes until soft, then add the rice and stir well. Pour in 1 litre (1¾ pints) of stock, add half the paprika, the saffron powder and seasoning. Stir well, then reduce the heat and add the chicken. Simmer uncovered for 25–30 minutes until the meat is cooked through and the rice is tender. Stir frequently to prevent the rice from sticking. Whenever the mixture becomes dry, stir in a little more stock. About 10 minutes before the end of the total cooking time, stir in the tomatoes, red pepper and peas. At the last minute, add the mussels and peeled prawns and heat through. Serve garnished with king prawns and lemon wedges and sprinkle with the remaining paprika.

SOUFFLE-TOPPED COD & SPINACH BAKE

Preparation time:	Serves:	Total cooking time:
10 minutes	4	35 minutes

450g (1 lb) smoked cod or haddock

275ml (½ pint) milk

50g (2 oz) butter

450g (1 lb) spinach, blanched

Salt and freshly ground black pepper

2 hard boiled eggs, chopped

25g (1 oz) plain flour

3 eggs, separated

Poach the fish in the milk until opaque and just cooked, then drain and reserve the milk. Roughly flake the fish, discarding any bones. Put to one side. Melt half the butter in a saucepan and add the spinach. Season well. Arrange the spinach on the base of a buttered ovenproof dish. Scatter the chopped eggs over the spinach and add the fish. Melt the remaining butter in a saucepan. Stir in the flour and cook for 3 minutes. Gradually add the reserved fish-flavoured milk, stirring continuously until the sauce is thick and smooth. Remove from the heat and beat in the egg yolks. Whisk the egg whites until stiff, then fold lightly into the sauce. Spread over the fish, making sure it covers the edges of the dish. Bake on the wire rack until the top is well risen and golden brown.

Function	Cooking time	Preheating	Shelf position
Conventional 190ºC	20 minutes	Yes	Second

FILLETS OF SOLE
WITH MUSHROOM STUFFING

Preparation time:	Serves:	Total cooking time:
10 minutes	4	20 minutes

175g (6 oz) button mushrooms

2 shallots

1 clove garlic

30ml (2 tbsp) fresh dill, finely chopped

150ml (5 fl oz) dry white wine

Salt and freshly ground black pepper

5ml (1 tsp) butter

25g (1 oz) Gruyère cheese, grated

4 Dover or lemon sole fillets, skinned

Finely chop the mushrooms, shallots and garlic. Dry fry the vegetables in a non-stick saucepan for 2–3 minutes. Remove from the heat and add the dill, 15ml (1 tbsp) of the wine and seasoning to taste. Lightly butter an oven-proof dish. Season the fish lightly, and place a quarter of the mushroom mixture on one end of each fillet. Roll up and place in the dish. Cover and bake in the oven until the fish is just cooked (10–15 minutes depending on the size of the fillets). Meanwhile, boil the wine in the saucepan until syrupy and reduced to 60ml (4 tbsp). Remove the fish from the oven, and drain the fish juices into the wine. Sprinkle the cheese over the fish and place under a very hot grill for 1 minute to melt the cheese. Serve accompanied by the sauce.

Function	Cooking time	Preheating	Shelf position
Fan heat 220°C	15 minutes	No	First

RAINBOW TROUT
WITH FENNEL STUFFING

Preparation time:	Serves:	Total cooking time:
15 minutes	4	20 minutes

4 medium rainbow trout, gutted

110g (4 oz) boiled rice

60ml (4 tbsp) fresh parsley, chopped

Half a fennel bulb, finely chopped

2 shallots, finely chopped

30ml (2 tbsp) pine nuts, toasted

Salt and freshly ground black pepper

50g (2 oz) butter, melted

60ml (4 tbsp) dry white wine

15ml (1 tbsp) olive oil

Lemon wedges to garnish

Wash the trout and trim the fins and tail. Mix the rice, parsley, fennel, shallots, pine nuts, seasoning and butter together, and use to stuff the trout. Place in an ovenproof dish. Pour the wine around the fish, and brush with a little oil. Cover with oiled silver foil and bake in the oven until cooked. Leave to rest, covered, for 5 minutes before serving with wedges of lemon.

Function	Cooking time	Preheating	Shelf position
Fan heat 200°C	20 minutes	No	First

LOBSTER THERMIDOR

LOBSTER THERMIDOR

Preparation time:	Serves:	Total cooking time:
20 minutes + infusing	4	35 minutes

2 x 700g (1½ lb) fresh lobsters, cooked*

275ml (½ pint) milk

Half a carrot

Half a small leek

Half an onion

1 bayleaf

Few peppercorns

50g (2 oz) butter

1 shallot, finely chopped

60ml (4 tbsp) white wine

15ml (1 tbsp) plain flour

Few sprigs of parsley

45ml (3 tbsp) Parmesan cheese, grated

Pinch of mustard powder

Salt

Pinch of paprika

*To cook the lobsters, bring a large saucepan of well salted water to the boil. Drop in the first lobster and return to the boil, then drop in the second lobster and bring to the boil again. Cook for 15 minutes on a full rolling boil. If you do not have a large enough pan to cook both lobsters at once, boil them separately. The lobsters must be fully immersed to cook properly.

Cut the lobsters in half lengthways and remove the meat from the shells. Chop the claw and head meat roughly, and cut the tail meat into slices.

Put the milk in a saucepan and add the carrot, leek, onion, bayleaf and peppercorns. Bring slowly to the boil. Remove from the heat, cover and leave to infuse for 15 minutes. Strain the milk and discard the flavourings. Melt half the butter in a saucepan and add the shallot. Sauté for 2–3 minutes until translucent. Add the wine and bring to the boil. Simmer for 5 minutes. Stir in the flour and cook for 2 minutes. Slowly pour in the flavoured milk, stirring continuously until the sauce thickens. Add the parsley, half the Parmesan, the lobster meat and the rest of the butter, cut into small pieces. Season with mustard powder, salt and a pinch of paprika. Spoon the mixture into the clean shells, and sprinkle with the remaining cheese. Grill to brown the surface and serve immediately.

Function	Cooking time	Preheating	Shelf position
Fan grill 200ºC	3–5 minutes	Yes	Third

TURBOT
WITH RED PEPPER COULIS

Preparation time:	Serves:	Total cooking time:
20 minutes	4	50 minutes

3 red peppers

150ml (5 fl oz) olive oil

50g (2 oz) shallots, peeled

2 cloves garlic, peeled

5ml (1 tsp) white wine vinegar, 55ml (2 fl oz) water

Salt and freshly ground black pepper

500g (1¼ lb) turbot fillet

5ml (1 tsp) Dijon mustard

8–10 fresh basil leaves

Cut the peppers in half and remove the stalks and seeds. Heat 55ml (2 fl oz) of the olive oil in an ovenproof casserole dish, and sauté the shallots until soft and translucent. Add the peppers and garlic, cover and cook in the oven for about 40 minutes until the peppers are soft. Remove the casserole from the oven, add the vinegar, and boil on the hob for about 10 seconds. Turn the mixture into a blender and liquidize to a smooth purée. Reserve 30ml (2 tbsp) of the remaining olive oil, and pour the rest into the puréed peppers. Process briefly to blend. Thin the purée with a little water to achieve a smooth, creamy consistency, and season with salt and pepper. Keep the sauce hot. Meanwhile, heat the reserved oil in a frying pan. Cut the turbot into 4 pieces and sear for a few seconds on each side. Season with salt and pepper. Transfer to a casserole dish, cover with a tight-fitting lid and cook in the oven for 7–10 minutes. Remove from the oven and leave to rest with the lid on for 5 minutes. Spread a little mustard over each piece of fish and top with a basil leaf. Spoon the hot pepper sauce onto 4 warmed plates and carefully arrange the turbot in the centre. Tear the remaining basil into pieces, and scatter over the sauce.

Sauce

Function	Cooking time	Preheating	Shelf position
Fan heat 180°C	40 minutes	No	First

Fish

Function	Cooking time	Preheating	Shelf position
Fan heat 180°C	7–10 minutes	No	First

WHOLE BASS BAKED IN COARSE SALT

Preparation time:	Serves:	Total cooking time:
5 minutes	4	40 minutes

900g (2 lb) fresh whole bass
1.8kg (4 lb) coarse sea salt
Lemon wedges
Extra virgin olive oil

Gut the fish. Leave the head on and do not scale. Trim the tail and fins, and remove the gills. Rinse the fish well, then pat dry. Spread 225g (8 oz) of the salt on the bottom of a baking dish. Place the fish on top, then cover completely with the remaining salt. Place the dish on the wire rack and bake in the centre of the oven for 40 minutes. Take out of the oven and brush away all the salt. Remove the skin carefully with a sharp knife, and discard. Remove the top fillet in neat pieces and transfer to 2 warmed plates. Remove the centre bones and discard, then transfer the bottom fillet to 2 further warmed plates. Serve immediately accompanied by lemon wedges and olive oil to drizzle over the fish.
NB: to enjoy this dish, the fish must be very fresh.

Function	Cooking time	Preheating	Shelf position
Conventional 230°C	40 minutes	Yes	Second

STUFFED ORANGE-GLAZED DUCK BREASTS

POULTRY & GAME

COUNTRY CRUMBLE

Preparation time:	Serves:	Total cooking time:
15 minutes	4	45 – 50 minutes

75g (3 oz) butter

450g (1 lb) chicken, cubed

150g (5 oz) plain wholemeal flour

425ml (3/4 pint) milk

Salt and freshly ground black pepper

10ml (2 tsp) fresh sage or 5ml (1 tsp) dried sage

1 leek and 1 carrot, sliced

110g (4 oz) button mushrooms and 50g (2 oz) peas

10ml (2 tsp) mustard powder and 5ml (1 tsp) paprika

110g (4 oz) mature Cheddar, grated and 25g (1 oz) muesli

15ml (1 tbsp) parsley, chopped

Melt 25g (1 oz) of the butter in a large saucepan, then add the chicken and fry for 5–6 minutes until lightly browned. Stir in 25g (1 oz) of the flour and cook for a further 3 minutes. Gradually stir in the milk and cook until the sauce is thick and smooth, stirring continuously. Season, then add the sage, leeks, carrots, mushrooms and peas, and simmer for 15 minutes, stirring occasionally. Meanwhile, make the crumble by rubbing the remaining flour and butter together until the mixture resembles fine breadcrumbs. Stir in the mustard, paprika, 75g (3 oz) of the cheese and the muesli. Remove the saucepan from the heat, add the remaining cheese and stir well. Pour into a 1.7 litre (3 pint) ovenproof dish, and sprinkle the crumble on top. Bake until golden brown, and garnish with parsley just before serving.

Function	Cooking time	Preheating	Shelf position
Fan heat 200ºC	20 –25 minutes	No	First

CHICKEN & MOZZARELLA EN PAPILLOTE

Preparation time:	Serves:	Total cooking time:
10 minutes	4	20 minutes

4 skinless chicken breast fillets

1 small ripe avocado, sliced

125g (4 1/2 oz) buffalo mozzarella cheese, sliced

4 sprigs fresh thyme

30ml (2 tbsp) fresh parsley

Salt and freshly ground black pepper

4 basil leaves

60ml (4 tbsp) dry white wine

4 cocktail sticks

4 large squares buttered greaseproof paper

Make a long slit in each chicken breast fillet to form a pocket. Divide the avocado and mozzarella between the 4 fillets, stuffing each one evenly. Secure the fillet with a cocktail stick to seal the pocket. Place each piece of chicken in the centre of a greaseproof paper square. Arrange the fresh herbs over the chicken and season well. Catch up the four corners of the paper to form a cup and spoon 15ml (1 tbsp) of wine over each chicken piece. Tightly fold the parcel and place carefully into a shallow ovenproof dish. Bake until the chicken is cooked through. Serve the chicken in its parcel along with the juices and accompany with seasonal vegetables.

Function	Cooking time	Preheating	Shelf position
Fan heat 200ºC	20 minutes	No	First

ROAST CHICKEN WITH APRICOT & ALMOND STUFFING

Preparation time:	Serves:	Total cooking time:
15 minutes	4	1 hour 40 – 50 mins

2kg (4.4 lb) fresh oven-ready chicken, without giblets

Half an onion and half a lemon, quartered

25g (1 oz) butter

Small bunch fresh parsley and thyme

Stuffing	2 rashers streaky bacon, chopped

25g (1 oz) flaked almonds

75g (3 oz) breadcrumbs

25g (1 oz) dried apricots, chopped

5ml (1 tsp) chopped parsley

Pinch of nutmeg

Salt and freshly ground black pepper

1 egg, beaten

To flavour the chicken, place the onion, lemon, butter and herbs into the body cavity. Set up the deep roasting tray and place the chicken on the wire rack. Roast in the oven, basting occasionally with the hot fat. If preferred, the chicken may be loosely covered with foil before roasting, but open the foil for the final 15–20 minutes to allow the bird to brown. The chicken is cooked when the juices run clear when a skewer is inserted between the thigh and the breast.

To make the stuffing, gently dry fry the bacon for 2–3 minutes. Add the almonds and cook for a further couple of minutes, stirring frequently. Mix with the remaining dry ingredients, then bind together with the egg. Leave to stand for 15 minutes. Roll spoonfuls of the mixture into balls

and place in a small dish. Cook with the chicken for the final 30 minutes. Serve the chicken with the stuffing, roast root vegetables and vichy carrots (see page 95), or for a change, a tossed green salad.

Function	Cooking time	Preheating	Shelf position
Auto roast 180°C	1 hr 40 – 50 mins	No	First

NB: allow 20 minutes per 450g (1 lb) plus 20 minutes

GRILLED CHICKEN WITH BOURSIN & HERB SAUCE

Preparation time:	Serves:	Total cooking time:
5 minutes	4	12 minutes

50g (2 oz) basil leaves

4 x 175g (6 oz) boneless chicken breasts with skin

Salt and freshly ground black pepper

60ml (4 tbsp) white wine vinegar

20ml (4 tsp) Dijon mustard and 1 clove garlic

175ml (6 fl oz) extra virgin olive oil

50g (2 oz) Boursin cheese

5ml (1 tsp) coarsely ground black peppercorns

Push 3 basil leaves under the skin of each chicken breast. Season well with salt and freshly ground black pepper. Grill for about 12 minutes, or until cooked, depending on thickness, turning halfway through the cooking time. Place the remaining basil leaves, vinegar, mustard, garlic, oil and Boursin in a food processor, and process until smooth. Stir in the peppercorns. Serve the chicken with the sauce and pasta ribbons.

Function	Cooking time	Preheating	Shelf position
Fan grill 180°C	12 minutes	No	Fourth

ROAST CHICKEN WITH APRICOT & ALMOND STUFFING

CHICKEN IN WINE & BRANDY SAUCE

Preparation time:	Serves:	Total cooking time:
25 minutes	4	50 minutes

30ml (2 tbsp) olive oil

4 chicken breasts, skinned

4 bacon rashers, chopped

200g (7 oz) shallots, chopped, 2 leeks and 2 carrots, sliced

45ml (3 tbsp) brandy

One 75cl bottle dry white wine

1 bayleaf, 1 sprig of thyme and a small bunch of parsley

3 cloves garlic, peeled

10ml (2 tsp) black peppercorns and 2 cloves

Salt and freshly ground black pepper

15ml (1 tbsp) plain flour

25g (1 oz) butter

Parsley to garnish

Heat the oil in a pan and gently fry the chicken breasts for 3–4 minutes to brown. Transfer to a flameproof casserole dish. Fry the bacon and vegetables for about 4 minutes to colour them. Add to the casserole dish. Pour the brandy into the hot frying pan and light it. Cover with a lid to extinguish the flames. In a separate saucepan, bring the wine to the boil. Pour a little into the frying pan to deglaze, scraping up all the cooking residues. Pour into the casserole together with the rest of the wine. Tie up the herbs, spices and garlic in muslin to form a bouquet garni, and add to the casserole. Bring to the boil, cover and transfer to the oven. Cook for about 30 minutes on the wire rack until the breasts are tender. Remove the chicken and vegetables and keep warm. Reduce the cooking liquor over a high heat until the flavour has intensified. Discard the bouquet garni. Mix the flour and softened butter to a paste. Whisk into the cooking liquor a little at a time until the sauce thickens. Pour the sauce over the meat and vegetables, and serve garnished with fresh parsley.

Function	Cooking time	Preheating	Shelf position
Conventional 180ºC	30 minutes	Yes	Third

CHICKEN, ALMOND & SPINACH CANNELLONI

Preparation time:	Serves:	Total cooking time:
30 minutes	4	50 minutes

350g (12 oz) frozen spinach, defrosted

30ml (2 tbsp) olive oil

1 large onion, finely chopped

1 clove garlic, crushed

1 chicken breast, minced

1 small green pepper, finely chopped

25g (1 oz) ground almonds

10g (1/2 oz) almonds, chopped

Salt and freshly ground black pepper

Pinch of nutmeg

20ml (4 tsp) fresh oregano, chopped

150ml (5 fl oz) vegetable stock

8 cannelloni tubes

400g (14 oz) tin chopped tomatoes

5ml (1 tsp) sugar

75g (3oz) mozzarella cheese, sliced

Chop the spinach finely. Heat 15ml (1 tbsp) of the oil in a large saucepan and gently fry half the onion with the garlic until soft. Stir in the minced chicken and green pepper and fry for 3–4 minutes. Stir in the spinach, almonds, seasoning, nutmeg, half the oregano and the stock, and cook for a further 3 minutes. Fill the cannelloni with the spinach mixture and place in a lightly oiled ovenproof dish. To make the sauce, heat the rest of the oil in a saucepan, and fry the rest of the onions for 4–5 minutes until lightly golden. Stir in the tomatoes, remaining herbs and sugar, bring to the boil and simmer for 5 minutes. Pour over the cannelloni and top with the sliced mozzarella. Bake in the oven until the pasta is cooked and the cheese has melted and started to bubble.

Function	Cooking time	Preheating	Shelf position
Fan heat 200°C	25–30 minutes	No	First

CHICKEN & SMOKED HAM LASAGNE

Preparation time:	Serves:	Total cooking time:
20 minutes	4	55–60 minutes

15ml (1 tbsp) olive oil

1 large onion, chopped

1 clove garlic, crushed

1 chicken breast, minced

2 sticks celery, finely chopped

400g (14 oz) tin chopped tomatoes

150ml (5 fl oz) chicken stock

30ml (2 tbsp) tomato purée

5ml (1 tsp) sugar

10ml (2 tsp) fresh oregano, chopped

25g (1 oz) butter

50g (2 oz) plain flour

570ml (1 pint) milk

Pinch of nutmeg

Salt and freshly ground black pepper

250g (9 oz) curd or cream cheese

175g (6 oz) lasagne verde

110g (4 oz) smoked ham, chopped

50g (2 oz) fresh Parmesan, grated

Heat the olive oil in a pan and sauté the onion, garlic, chicken and celery until lightly golden. Stir in the tomatoes, stock, purée, sugar and herbs. Bring to the boil, reduce the heat, cover and simmer for 5 minutes. Meanwhile, to make the sauce, melt the butter in a saucepan, stir in the flour and cook for 2 minutes. Whisk in the milk, nutmeg and seasoning, and cook until thick and smooth, stirring continuously. Remove from the heat and add the cheese. Whisk again until smooth and creamy. Cover the base of a deep-sided lasagne dish with a little of the sauce. Place a layer of lasagne sheets on top, and cover them with some of the chicken and tomato mixture and a sprinkling of ham. Repeat the process, ending with a layer of the white sauce. Top with grated Parmesan and bake on the wire rack until the lasagne is cooked and the topping is golden brown.

Function	Cooking time	Preheating	Shelf position
Conventional 200°C	35–40 minutes	Yes	Second

CHICKEN IN WINE & BRANDY SAUCE

CHICKEN & COURGETTE RISOTTO

Preparation time:	Serves:	Total cooking time:
15 minutes	4	1 hour 20 minutes

75g (3 oz) butter

1 onion, chopped

500g (1¼ lb) courgettes, thinly sliced

350g (12 oz) arborio rice

200ml (7 fl oz) dry white wine

1 litre (1¾ pints) hot chicken stock

4 sprigs fresh thyme

2 skinless chicken breasts, cubed

2 tomatoes, skinned and chopped

Salt and freshly ground black pepper

60ml (4 tbsp) fresh parsley, chopped

45ml (3 tbsp) freshly grated Parmesan

Melt half the butter in a large heatproof casserole dish. Gently fry the onion until soft and translucent, but do not allow to colour. Add the courgettes and rice, and stir well to coat evenly in butter. Pour in the wine and bring to the boil. Stir in the chicken stock, thyme, chicken, tomatoes and seasoning. Bring to the boil, cover with a tight-fitting lid and transfer to the oven. Cook in the oven for about an hour until the rice has softened and has absorbed most of the liquid. Stir in the remaining butter, parsley and Parmesan, and serve immediately.

Function	Cooking time	Preheating	Shelf position
Fan heat 190ºC	1 hour	No	First

THAI RED CHICKEN CURRY

Preparation time:	Serves:	Total cooking time:
10 minutes	4	35 minutes

50g (2 oz) coconut cream

45ml (3 tbsp) red curry paste

400g (14 oz) chicken breast

350ml (12 fl oz) coconut milk

22.5ml (1½ tbsp) Thai fish sauce

5ml (1 tsp) sugar

150g (5 oz) aubergine, cubed

Handful of basil leaves

2–3 fresh red chillies, finely sliced

Heat the coconut cream in a frying pan until it begins to have an oily sheen. Mix in the curry paste and stir well. Cut the chicken into pieces and cook with the paste mixture until the meat is opaque. Stir in the coconut milk, fish sauce and sugar. Bring to the boil and stir in the cubed aubergine. Transfer the ingredients to a heatproof casserole dish. Cover with a tight-fitting lid and bake until the chicken is tender. Stir in the basil and chillies. Serve with fragrant Thai rice.

Function	Cooking time	Preheating	Shelf position
Fan heat 180ºC	20 minutes	No	First

ORIENTAL WHOLE ROAST DUCKLING

Preparation time:	Serves:	Total cooking time:
5 minutes + marinading	4	2 hours

150ml (5 fl oz) dry sherry

45ml (3 tbsp) soy sauce

30ml (2 tbsp) clear honey

15ml (1 tbsp) sherry vinegar

1 celery stalk, sliced

1 clove garlic, crushed

10g (1/2 oz) fresh root ginger, finely chopped

2.3 kg (5 lb) duckling

10ml (2 tsp) salt

Put all the ingredients except the duckling and the salt into a saucepan. Bring to the boil, reduce the heat and simmer gently for 10 minutes. Cool the marinade, strain and discard the vegetables. Remove any loose fat from the duck cavity and discard. Pierce the duck all over with a cocktail stick or sharp knife. Place in a shallow dish, breast side down. Pour the marinade over the duck, cover and leave in the refrigerator for 24 hours, turning occasionally. Dry the duck thoroughly and rub the skin well with salt. Set up the deep roasting tray, place the duckling in the centre and roast in the oven. Baste occasionally, until the bird is tender and the juices run clear when a fine skewer is inserted into the thigh. Serve with stir-fried vegetables.

Function	Cooking time	Preheating	Shelf position
Auto roast 175ºC	1 hr 40–50 mins	No	First

ROAST GOOSE WITH GOOSEBERRY SAUCE

Preparation time:	Serves:	Total cooking time:
10 minutes	6–8	3 hours

4kg (9 lb) goose

Bunch fresh mixed herbs

Salt

Sauce   225g (8 oz) gooseberries, fresh or frozen

25g (1 oz) butter

30–60ml (2–4 tbsp) sugar

Remove the giblets and rinse the goose inside and out. Fill the body cavity with the mixed herbs. Prick the skin carefully, without piercing the meat, to allow the fat to escape. Season well with salt. Set up the deep roasting tray and place the bird on the wire rack. Loosely cover with foil. Roast, basting occasionally, until the goose is tender and the juices run clear when the flesh is pierced with a fine skewer. Drain off the fat halfway through the cooking time. Leave the meat to rest, covered, in a warm place for 15 minutes before carving.

To make the sauce, top and tail the gooseberries. Stew the fruit in 30ml (2 tbsp) of water until soft. Purée, then add the butter and sugar to taste, depending on the sourness of the gooseberries. Serve the goose with the sauce, roast potatoes and brussels sprouts.

Function	Cooking time	Preheating	Shelf position
Fan heat 160ºC	2 hrs 45 – 3 hrs	No	First

BREAST OF DUCK WITH MADEIRA SAUCE

STUFFED ORANGE-GLAZED DUCK BREASTS

Preparation time:	Serves:	Total cooking time:
20 minutes	4	12 – 15 minutes

4 duck breasts

1 orange, zest and juice and 15ml (1 tbsp) orange marmalade

30ml (2 tbsp) Cointreau

50g (2 oz) cooked rice

1 small onion and 1 stick celery, finely chopped

4 ready to eat dried apricots, chopped

15ml (1 tbsp) pine nuts, chopped

15ml (1 tbsp) parsley, chopped

Salt and freshly ground black pepper

4 cocktail sticks

Score the skin of the duck breasts diagonally. Make a deep pocket in each duck breast. In a bowl, mix together the orange zest, half the juice, the marmalade and Cointreau. Brush the duck breasts generously all over with the mixture. Add the remaining ingredients to the bowl and bind together with the rest of the orange juice. Spoon the stuffing mixture into the pockets of the duck breasts. Secure the filling by closing the pockets and piercing with cocktail sticks. Arrange the duck breasts on the wire rack with the deep roasting tray underneath. Cook under a hot grill, turning occasionally, according to taste. Baste twice during cooking period using the remaining marmalade mixture. When cooked, remove from the oven and leave to rest in a warm place for 5 minutes before serving.

Function	Cooking time	Preheating	Shelf position
Fan grill 200ºC	12–15 minutes	Yes	Third

BREAST OF DUCK WITH MADEIRA SAUCE

Preparation time:	Serves:	Total cooking time:
10 minutes	4	30 minutes

4 duck breasts on the bone

30ml (2 tbsp) butter

15ml (1 tbsp) olive oil

175ml (6 fl oz) Madeira

2 shallots, chopped

15ml (1 tbsp) tomato purée

570ml (1 pint) fresh chicken stock

Salt and freshly ground black pepper

15ml (1 tbsp) plain flour

30ml (2 tbsp) chopped fresh herbs (rosemary, basil, thyme)

16 black olives, pitted

Remove the bones from the duck breasts and chop into small pieces. Heat half the butter with the olive oil in a large frying pan, and add the duck bones. Sauté until browned. Remove the excess fat from the pan and deglaze with 150ml (5 fl oz) Madeira, scraping the pan to loosen any sediment. Add the shallots, tomato purée and the rest of the wine, then flambé. When the flames subside, add the stock, bring to the boil and reduce by half. Strain through a fine sieve and return to the hob in a clean saucepan. Season to taste. Soften the remaining butter and mix with the flour to form a smooth paste. Gradually whisk into the sauce and cook until the sauce is smooth and coats the back of the spoon. Put to one side.

Remove the tendons from the duck breasts and press the chopped herbs onto the meat. Cook under a preheated grill for about 5 minutes on each side, depending on the thickness, until browned on the outside and slightly pink in the centre. Cover and leave to rest in a warm place for 5–10 minutes before carving diagonally into slices. Just before serving, gently reheat the sauce and add the olives. Spoon a pool of sauce onto each warm plate. Arrange the slices of duck over the sauce and spoon a little more sauce over the meat. Serve immediately, garnished if liked with deep-fried, battered onion slices.

Function	Cooking time	Preheating	Shelf position
Fan grill 200°C	10 minutes	Yes	Fourth

BRAISED PHEASANTS IN CHESTNUT MUSHROOM SAUCE

Preparation time:	Serves:	Total cooking time:
15 minutes	4	2 hours

A brace of pheasants, jointed

Salt and freshly ground black pepper

100g (3¹/₂ oz) butter

15ml (1 tbsp) olive oil

12 shallots, peeled

350g (12 oz) streaky bacon, chopped

2 cloves garlic, finely chopped

275ml (¹/₂ pint) pheasant or chicken stock

2 bayleaves and a few sprigs fresh thyme

275ml (¹/₂ pint) dry white wine

275ml (¹/₂ pint) Madeira

225g (8 oz) chestnut mushrooms, sliced

40g (1¹/₂ oz) plain flour

Season the pheasant pieces with salt and pepper. Heat half the butter with the oil in a frying pan and sauté the pheasant until golden brown. Transfer to a large ovenproof casserole dish. Sauté the shallots and bacon until golden brown. Remove from the pan and reserve. Sauté the garlic for 1 minute, then pour the stock into the pan and bring to the boil, scraping up the juices from the bottom of the pan. Pour over the pheasant pieces and add the herbs and wine. Cover and cook in the oven for 1 hour, then add the reserved shallots and bacon, together with the mushrooms. Return to the oven and cook for a further 30 minutes, until the pheasant is very tender. Mix the rest of the butter and flour together to a paste. Transfer the pheasant pieces and vegetables to a warmed serving dish, cover and keep warm. Bring the cooking liquid to the boil on the hob, and reduce by a third. Gradually whisk in the flour paste until the sauce thickens. Pour some of the sauce over the pheasant and vegetables, and serve the remainder in a sauce boat. Serve with root vegetables.

Function	Cooking time	Preheating	Shelf position
Fan heat 170°C	1 hour 30 mins	No	First

BRAISED PHEASANTS IN CHESTNUT MUSHROOM SAUCE

BRAISED VENISON IN REDCURRANT SAUCE

Preparation time:	Serves:	Total cooking time:
20 minutes + marinading	4	2 hours 15 mins

350g (12 oz) shoulder of venison, diced

6 black peppercorns, 1 bayleaf and 1 sprig fresh thyme

1 strip orange peel and 1 carrot, diced

1 onion, roughly chopped and 3 garlic cloves, chopped

1 stick celery, sliced

110g (4 oz) smoked streaky bacon, chopped

275ml (½ pint) red wine

30ml (2 tbsp) olive oil

Salt and freshly ground black pepper

15ml (1 tbsp) tomato purée

15ml (1 tbsp) redcurrant jelly

Place the venison, peppercorns, bayleaf, thyme, orange peel, carrot, onion, garlic, celery, bacon and red wine into a bowl. Cover and leave to marinate overnight in the refrigerator. Drain the venison and vegetables and pat dry, reserving the flavoured wine for later. In a non-stick pan, heat the oil over a high heat. Sauté the venison, vegetables and bacon for about 5 minutes, until well coloured. Add the seasoning, tomato purée and reserved wine. Bring to the boil for 1 minute. Place the mixture into a casserole dish and cover with a tight-fitting lid. Braise in the oven until the venison is very tender. Strain the juices into a large saucepan and reduce by about a third. Add the redcurrant jelly, stir in the venison and vegetables and reheat gently. Serve with parsnip purée and sautéed potatoes.

Function	Cooking time	Preheating	Shelf position
Fan heat 130ºC	2 hours	No	First

AROMATIC RABBIT CASSEROLE

Preparation time:	Serves:	Total cooking time:
15 minutes	4	1 hour 30 minutes

Good pinch of saffron threads

15ml (1 tbsp) olive oil

1 large red onion, sliced

700g (1½ lb) rabbit pieces, boned

30ml (2 tbsp) seasoned flour

60ml (4 tbsp) dried apricots

110g (4 oz) long grain rice, washed

5cm (2 inch) cinnamon stick

2 bayleaves

570ml (1 pint) chicken or rabbit stock

Salt and freshly ground black pepper

Soak the saffron threads in 30ml (2 tbsp) of boiling water. Heat the oil in a heatproof casserole dish and sauté the onions until soft. Coat the rabbit pieces in the seasoned flour and brown with the onions for 3–4 minutes. Add the remaining ingredients, including the saffron and its liquid and stir, scraping any sediment from the bottom of the pan. Cover with a tight-fitting lid and transfer to the oven. Cook until the rabbit is tender and the rice has cooked and absorbed most of the liquid.

Function	Cooking time	Preheating	Shelf position
Fan heat 170ºC	1 hour 15 mins	No	First

ROAST TURKEY

CHRISTMAS DINNER: TO SERVE EIGHT

ROAST TURKEY

Preparation time:	Total cooking time:
10 minutes + any defrosting	3¹/₄ – 3¹/₂ hours

4Kg (8.8 lb) oven-ready turkey

Chestnut stuffing (see page 52)

1 onion, quartered

25 – 50g (1 – 2 oz) butter

225g (8 oz) streaky bacon (optional)

Remove the giblets from the turkey and reserve. Wash the bird inside and out, and dry well. Stuff the neck end of the turkey with chestnut stuffing, allowing 450g (1 lb) of stuffing for a bird of up to 6.3kg (14 lb), or twice this for a larger bird. Place the quartered onion inside the body cavity. Truss the turkey to give it a good shape. Rub generously with butter and cover the breast with strips of bacon. Weigh the bird, complete with stuffing, to calculate the cooking time according to the recommendations. Remember that the turkey should be ready 30 minutes before you intend to serve, to give it time to rest. Wrap the bird in foil to prevent the flesh drying and the skin hardening. Place the turkey in the oven and roast for the appropriate time. For best results, unwrap the foil for the last 30 minutes, baste the bird, and continue cooking uncovered for the bacon to crisp. To test whether the bird is ready, pierce the thigh flesh with a skewer. The juices should run clear. When cooked, leave the turkey to rest, covered, for 30 minutes before carving. Serve with the stuffing, bacon rolls, bread sauce and seasonal vegetables.

Function	Cooking time	Preheating	Shelf position
Auto roast 160°C	3¹/₄ – 3¹/₂ hours	No	First

Allow 20 minutes per 450g (1 lb) stuffed weight plus 20 minutes

NB: it is vital that the turkey (and indeed all other poultry) is thawed completely. Thawing at room temperature is best, then refrigerate if the bird is not to be cooked immediately. Stuffing the turkey is safe provided both the bird and the stuffing are completely defrosted, allowing the heat to penetrate quickly.

Guide to thawing times at room temperature (20°C)			
1.4kg (3 lb)	9 hours	2.3kg (5 lb)	15 hours
4.5kg (10 lb)	18 hours	6.8kg (15 lb)	24 hours
9kg (20 lb)	30 hours		

CHESTNUT STUFFING

Preparation time:	Sufficient for a:
10 minutes	4.5kg (10 lb) turkey

25g (1 oz) butter

Half an onion, finely chopped

1 turkey liver, finely chopped (optional)

110g (4 oz) bacon, rinded and finely chopped

225g (8 oz) chestnut purée*

110g (4 oz) fresh breadcrumbs

110g (4 oz) best quality pork sausage meat

Grated rind of 1 lemon

1 egg, beaten

15ml (1 tbsp) fresh parsley, chopped

Salt and freshly ground black pepper

Melt the butter in a frying pan and add the onions, turkey liver and bacon. Cook for approximately 5 minutes until the onion is translucent. Combine with all the remaining ingredients and season to taste. Use to stuff the neck cavity of the turkey.

*Chestnut purée may be made from fresh, dried or tinned chestnuts, or use tinned unsweetened purée.

BACON ROLLS

Preparation time:
5 minutes

8 chipolata sausages

16 rashers smoked streaky bacon

Remove the rind from the bacon. Cut the sausages in half and wrap each one in a rasher of bacon. Place the rolls on a lightly oiled baking tray or around the turkey, and cook for about 30 minutes.

Function	Cooking time	Preheating	Shelf position
Fan heat 180ºC	30 minutes	No	First

TRADITIONAL BREAD SAUCE

Preparation time:	Total cooking time:
5 minutes + infusing	20 minutes

1 large onion, halved

4 cloves, 1 bayleaf

570ml (1 pint) milk

Salt and freshly ground black pepper

110g (4 oz) fresh white breadcrumbs

25g (1 oz) butter and 15ml (1 tbsp) double cream

Stud the onion with the cloves and place in a saucepan with the bayleaf, milk and seasoning. Bring to the boil, then leave the covered pan in a warm place to infuse for 2 hours. Remove the onion and bayleaf, and stir in the breadcrumbs and butter. Cook over a gentle heat for 15 minutes, stirring occasionally, until the crumbs have swollen and thickened the sauce. Beat in the cream and pour into a warmed jug to serve.

CHRISTMAS JALOUSIE
A DELICIOUS VEGETARIAN ALTERNATIVE TO ROAST TURKEY

Preparation time:	Total cooking time:
25 minutes	55 minutes

50g (2 oz) butter

1 large onion, finely chopped

2 cloves garlic, crushed

225g (8 oz) carrots, grated

Few sprigs of fresh thyme

225g (8 oz) wild and cultivated mushrooms
(chanterelle, trompettes de mort, chestnut)

30ml (2 tbsp) olive oil

2 drops truffle oil (optional)

30ml (2 tbsp) fresh parsley, chopped

30ml (2 tbsp) passata sauce

175g (6 oz) tin whole peeled chestnuts

100g (4 oz) cream cheese

Salt and freshly ground black pepper

500g (1 lb 2 oz) puff pastry

Beaten egg to glaze

Melt the butter in a large frying pan and fry the onion until soft and translucent. Add the garlic, carrots and thyme, and sauté for about 10 minutes until the liquid from the carrots has evaporated. Leave to cool. Meanwhile, slice the mushrooms. In a separate pan, heat the olive oil and truffle oil, if using, and sauté the mushrooms for 2–3 minutes. Stir in the parsley, passata and chestnuts, and leave to cool. Mix the cream cheese into the carrot mixture, then fold in the mushrooms and sauce. Roll out the pastry on a lightly floured surface to a rectangle 45 x 38cm (18 x 15 inches). Pile the cooled mixture down the centre. Cut the pastry at an angle on either side in wide bands, and bring them up and over the filling, alternating to form a plait. Brush with beaten egg and bake until well risen and golden brown.

Function	Cooking time	Preheating	Shelf position
Fan heat 220ºC	40 minutes	Yes	Second

CELEBRATION MOUSSE

Preparation time:
5 minutes + chilling

450g (1 lb) plain chocolate

60ml (4 tbsp) rum

6 eggs, separated

275ml (½ pint) double cream, whipped

Whipped cream and chocolate curls to decorate

Break the chocolate into pieces and melt slowly in a bowl over a pan of simmering water. Stir until smooth. Remove from the heat and allow to cool slightly before stirring in the rum. Whisk the egg yolks until creamy, and gradually stir into the chocolate. Gently fold in the cream. Whisk the egg whites until stiff, and carefully fold into the chocolate mixture. Turn into 8 individual ramekin dishes or a 1.75 litre (3 pint) soufflé dish. Chill for 3–4 hours, preferably overnight. Remove from the refrigerator 1 hour before serving, and decorate with whipped cream and chocolate curls.

CHRISTMAS PUDDING

Preparation time:	Makes a:	Total cooking time:
15 minutes + standing	900g (2 lb) pudding	8 hrs + reheating

175g (6 oz) plain flour

5ml (1 tsp) mixed spice

2.5ml (½ tsp) cinnamon

2.5ml (½ tsp) grated nutmeg

110g (4 oz) breadcrumbs

110g (4 oz) vegetable suet

110g (4 oz) demerara sugar

25g (1 oz) flaked almonds

175g (6 oz) sultanas

175g (6 oz) raisins

175g (6 oz) currants

50g (2 oz) glacé cherries

1 apple, grated

1 lemon rind, grated

1 orange rind, grated

30ml (2 tbsp) brandy

2 eggs, beaten

5ml (1 tsp) treacle

110–150ml (4–5 fl oz) cider

Sift the flour and spices into a large bowl. Stir in the breadcrumbs, suet, sugar and nuts. Add the fruits, make a well in the centre, and pour in the brandy, beaten eggs and treacle. Combine thoroughly. Gradually add the cider, mixing until a smooth dropping consistency is obtained. Cover the bowl and leave to stand for 24 hours. The next day, lightly butter a 1.2 litre (2 pint) pudding basin and pack in the mixture firmly. Cover the basin with a double layer of greaseproof paper, pleated down the middle, then with a layer of foil. Tie securely with string. Place the pudding in a steamer set over a pan of simmering water and steam for 8 hours, topping up with boiling water whenever necessary. Remove the basin from the pan and allow the pudding to cool completely. Remove the greaseproof paper and foil, and replace with fresh sheets. Store in a cool, dry place for at least 1 month before eating. To serve, steam the pudding for 3–4 hours, then turn onto a warmed dish and serve with brandy or rum butter. Any remaining pudding may be reheated on Boxing Day by wrapping in foil and heating in a moderate oven (180°C) for 20–30 minutes.

BRANDY OR RUM BUTTER

Preparation time:
5 minutes

110g (4 oz) unsalted butter, softened

110g (4 oz) icing sugar, sifted

25g (1 oz) ground almonds

30ml (2 tbsp) brandy or rum

60ml (4 tbsp) double cream

Cream the butter and icing sugar together. Stir in the ground almonds and brandy or rum, mixing until smooth. Gently stir in the double cream, cover and refrigerate for up to 3 days. Remove from the refrigerator 30 minutes before serving with Christmas pudding.

CHRISTMAS PUDDING

ROAST BEEF AND YORKSHIRE PUDDINGS

BEEF, PORK & LAMB

ROAST BEEF

Preparation time:
5 minutes

Total cooking time:
See below

1 joint of beef

Salt and freshly ground black pepper

Allow the meat to reach room temperature. Wipe down and trim if necessary, then weigh and calculate the cooking time. Set up the deep roasting tray, place the joint on the wire rack, with the thickest layer of fat uppermost, and rub salt and pepper into the fat. Roast the meat in the oven, basting from time to time with the meat juices. Remove from the oven, cover and leave to rest in a warm place for 20 minutes before carving. Serve accompanied by Yorkshire pudding, horseradish sauce, roast potatoes and a selection of fresh, seasonal vegetables.

Function	Cooking time	Preheating	Shelf position
Auto roast 180°C	See below	No	First

Time: 20 minutes per 450g (1lb) plus 25 minutes, or use the Roast probe:

Roast probe	Rare	Medium	Well done
	60 – 65°C	65 – 75°C	75 – 80°C

YORKSHIRE PUDDINGS

Preparation time:
5 minutes

Serves:
4

Total cooking time:
20 – 30 minutes

Beef fat from the roasting joint, or oil

110g (4 oz) plain flour, sifted

Salt

2 eggs, lightly whisked

150ml (5 fl oz) milk

This quantity will be sufficient for a 4-cup Yorkshire pudding tin, 10–12 patty tins or a 20cm (8 inch) square dish. Fill each cup of the Yorkshire pudding tin with 10–15ml (2–3 tsp) of fat or oil; use 5–10ml (1–2 tsp) in each of the individual patty tins or use 30–45ml (2–3 tbsp) in the square dish. Place in the preheated oven until very hot. Meanwhile, put the flour and salt in a mixing bowl and make a well in the centre. Pour in the eggs, and whisk until the batter is smooth. Add the milk gradually, mixing well after each addition. Pour the batter into the hot tins and cook for 15–20 minutes until well risen and golden. NB: if you are roasting in the oven, increase the temperature to 220°C 10 minutes before the meat is cooked, and put the greased tins in the oven to heat. Remove the meat, cover and leave to rest. Pour the batter into the smoking hot tins and cook as above.

Function	Cooking time	Preheating	Shelf position
Fan heat 200°C or Conventional 220°C	15 – 20 minutes	Yes	First

BŒUF EN CROUTE

Preparation time:	Serves:	Total cooking time:
15 minutes	4 – 6	30 minutes

450g (1 lb) fillet beef, trimmed

5ml (1 tsp) freshly ground black pepper

15ml (1 tbsp) olive oil

40g (1½ oz) shallots, finely chopped

15ml (1 tbsp) Dijon mustard

375g (13 oz) puff pastry

150g (5oz) mushrooms, finely chopped

1 egg, beaten

Tie the fillet with string in 3–4 places, so that it retains its shape when seared. Season with freshly ground black pepper. Heat the oil in a frying pan and sear the beef all over to brown. Remove the meat from the pan and reserve. Sauté the shallots until soft and translucent, then put to one side. Remove the ties from the beef and cover all over with Dijon mustard. Roll out the pastry to an oblong measuring 25 x 45.5cm (10 x 18 inch). Mix the shallots and mushrooms together and spread the mixture down the centre of the pastry. Lay the fillet of beef on top. Brush the edges of the pastry with egg and fold over. Turn the parcel over so that the seam is underneath, and seal the ends under the meat. Glaze with the remaining egg. Place on a small baking tray and place in the oven on the wire rack. Bake until the pastry is well risen and golden brown. Leave to stand in a warm place for 5 minutes before serving.

Function	Cooking time	Preheating	Shelf position
Conventional 200°C	20 – 30 minutes	Yes	Second

CARBONNADE OF BEEF

Preparation time:	Serves:	Total cooking time:
10 minutes	4	1 hour 30 mins

500g (1 lb 2 oz) lean braising steak, cubed

25g (1 oz) seasoned flour

30ml (2 tbsp) vegetable oil

2 large onions, sliced

50g (2 oz) chopped bacon

1 clove garlic, crushed

200ml (7 fl oz) beef stock

350ml (12 fl oz) stout

5ml (1 tsp) dark brown sugar

10ml (2 tsp) red wine vinegar

1 bayleaf

Salt and freshly ground black pepper

Toss the steak in the seasoned flour. Heat half the oil in a frying pan and seal the meat. Transfer to a casserole dish. Heat the remaining oil in the frying pan and gently sauté the onions and bacon until golden brown, adding the garlic halfway through. Add to the dish with the beef. Pour the beef stock and stout into the frying pan and bring to the boil, scraping any sediment from the bottom of the pan. Pour the stock into the casserole and add the remaining ingredients. Cover with a lid and cook until the beef is tender and the sauce has thickened.

Function	Cooking time	Preheating	Shelf position
Fan heat 190°C	1 hr 15 – 30 mins	No	First

BŒUF EN CROUTE

BEEF, PORK & LAMB

BEEF & OXTAIL STEW

Preparation time:	Serves:	Total cooking time:
20 minutes	4 – 6	3 – 4 hours

1 oxtail, trimmed of fat

45ml (3 tbsp) seasoned flour

700g (1½ lb) braising or stewing steak

50g (2 oz) butter

3 rashers streaky bacon, chopped

4 onions, sliced and 4 large carrots, cut into thirds

3 cloves garlic, crushed

55ml (2 fl oz) Cognac

¾ bottle red wine

570ml (1 pint) rich beef stock

2.5ml (½ tsp) salt and a bouquet garni

225g (8oz) button mushrooms

8 shallots, peeled

Wash the oxtail, dab dry and coat lightly in the seasoned flour, along with the steak. Melt the butter in a large flameproof casserole dish and fry the bacon gently. Add the oxtail and steak, and fry until the pieces are golden brown. Remove the meat and keep warm, then gently fry the onions and carrots. Add the crushed garlic and return the meat to the casserole. Cook over a moderate heat for 5 minutes. Add the Cognac and flambé, then douse the flames by pouring in the wine. Stir in the stock, salt and bouquet garni, cover and cook in the oven for 2 hours. Add the mushrooms and shallots, and cook for a further hour or until the meat is tender. Skim off any impurities. Serve with mashed potatoes and braised red cabbage (see page 94).

Function	Cooking time	Preheating	Shelf position
Fan heat 120°C	3 – 4 hours	No	First

CHILLI CON CARNE

Preparation time:	Serves:	Total cooking time:
15 minutes	4 – 6	1 hour 20 minutes

30ml (2 tbsp) olive oil

1 onion, chopped and 1 clove garlic, crushed

Half a red pepper and half a green pepper, chopped

110g (4 oz) bacon, chopped

450g (1 lb) extra lean minced beef

5ml (1 tsp) ground ginger and 2.5ml (½ tsp) ground cumin

5 – 10ml (1 – 2 tsp) chilli powder

150ml (5 fl oz) beef stock and 150ml (5 fl oz) red wine

2 bayleaves

400g (14 oz) tin chopped tomatoes

15ml (1 tbsp) tomato purée

400g (14 oz) tin kidney beans

Salt and freshly ground black pepper

15ml (1 tbsp) plain flour

Fresh parsley to garnish

Heat the oil in a frying pan and sauté the onion, garlic, peppers and bacon until soft. Add the minced beef and sauté until well browned. Stir in the spices and cook for 1 minute. Add the stock, wine, bayleaves, tomatoes, purée, kidney beans and seasoning, and bring to the boil, stirring continuously. Mix the flour to a paste with a little cold water and stir into the chilli. Spoon into an ovenproof casserole dish, cover and bake on the wire rack for 1 hour or until rich and creamy. Just before serving, stir in some chopped parsley. Serve with brown rice.

Function	Cooking time	Preheating	Shelf position
Conventional 200°C	1 hour	Yes	Second

HUNGARIAN GOULASH

Preparation time:	Serves:	Total cooking time:
10 minutes	4	2 hours 15 mins

30ml (2 tbsp) olive oil

450g (1 lb) chuck steak, cubed

2 large onions, chopped and 1 clove garlic, crushed

10ml (2 tsp) caraway seeds

30ml (2 tbsp) paprika

5ml (1 tsp) nutmeg, grated

30ml (2 tbsp) plain flour

400g (14 oz) tin chopped tomatoes

275ml (½ pint) beef stock

1 bouquet garni

Salt and freshly ground black pepper

1 red pepper, cut into strips

150ml (¼ pint) soured cream

Heat the oil in a frying pan and brown the steak. Remove from the pan with a slotted spoon and place in a casserole dish. Add the onions and garlic to the pan and fry until lightly golden. Mix in the caraway seeds, paprika, nutmeg and flour and cook for 1–2 minutes. Stir in the tomatoes and the juice and cook for a further 2 minutes, stirring continuously. Add the stock and bouquet garni, and season with salt and pepper. Pour the sauce over the meat. Cover with a tight-fitting lid and cook on the wire rack until the meat is very tender. About 45 minutes before the end of the cooking time, stir in the strips of red pepper. Just before serving, add the soured cream and sprinkle with a little paprika.

Function	Cooking time	Preheating	Shelf position
Conventional 180ºC	2 hours	No	Second

STEAK WITH DIJONNAISE SAUCE

Preparation time:	Serves:	Total cooking time:
5 minutes + marinading	4	10 minutes

4 x 175g (6 oz) fillet steaks

60ml (4 tbsp) Drambuie

25g (1 oz) butter

50g (2 oz) onion, finely chopped

50g (2 oz) crème fraîche

10ml (2 tsp) Dijon mustard

10ml (2 tsp) black peppercorns, crushed

10ml (2 tsp) lemon juice

30ml (2 tbsp) chopped parsley

Place the steaks in a shallow dish with the Drambuie and marinate for at least 10 minutes, turning occasionally. Remove the steaks and pat them dry, reserving the alcohol for later. Place the fillets under the preheated grill and cook for several minutes on each side, according to taste. Meanwhile, to make the sauce, melt the butter in a saucepan. Add the onions and fry for a few minutes, not forgetting to check the steaks in the meantime. Reduce the heat and add the crème fraîche, reserved Drambuie, mustard, peppercorns and the lemon juice, mixing well. Stir in the parsley and serve with the grilled steaks. Steak is also delicious served with Stroganoff sauce (see page 140).

Function	Cooking time	Preheating	Shelf position
Fan grill 220ºC	10 minutes	Yes	Fourth/fifth

VINTAGE STEAK & KIDNEY PIE

Preparation time:	Serves:	Total cooking time:
15 minutes + marinading/chilling	4 – 6	1 hour 50 minutes

450g (1 lb) rump steak, cubed

275ml (½ pint) red wine

225g (8 oz) lamb's kidneys

1 large onion, chopped

30ml (2 tbsp) olive oil

30ml (2 tbsp) seasoned flour

Fresh bouquet garni (parsley, thyme, bayleaf)

275ml (½ pint) beef stock

Salt and freshly ground black pepper

Pastry   225g (8 oz) plain flour

110g (4 oz) butter

60ml (4 tbsp) cold water

Beaten egg to glaze

Place the steak in a bowl and marinate in the wine for 1 hour. Snip out the centre core from the kidneys and cut into pieces. Fry the onion in hot oil until golden brown. Drain the marinade from the meat and reserve. Dry the steak thoroughly and toss in the seasoned flour, shaking off any excess. Keep the excess flour to coat the kidneys later. Add the steak to the onions and fry until brown on all sides. Stir in the reserved marinade, the bouquet garni and stock. Bring to the boil, reduce the heat, cover and simmer gently for 1 hour until the beef is tender. About halfway through cooking, toss the kidney in flour and sauté in a little hot oil for 3–4 minutes, then add to the pan. Season to taste. Remove from the heat, cool and then chill, ideally overnight.

To make the pastry, sift the flour and a pinch of salt into a bowl. Rub in the butter until the mixture resembles fine breadcrumbs. Mix in enough water to give a fairly firm dough. Roll out ⅔ of the pastry on a floured surface, and use to line a 17.5 x 25cm (7 x 10 inch) pie dish. Fill the dish with the steak and kidney mixture. Cover with the remaining pastry, sealing the edges well. Glaze the top of the pie with beaten egg, and make two slits in the centre for the steam to escape. Bake on the wire rack until the pastry is crisp and golden.

Function	Cooking time	Preheating	Shelf position
Conventional 220°C	30 – 35 minutes	Yes	Second

PAN-FRIED STEAK
WITH PORT & DOLCELATTE SAUCE

Preparation time:	Serves:	Total cooking time:
10 minutes	4	5 minutes

4 x 150–175g (5–6 oz) thick-cut fillet steaks

225g (8 oz) dolcelatte

30ml (2 tbsp) oil

Salt and freshly ground pepper

110ml (4 fl oz) port and 150ml (¼ pint) soured cream

Using a sharp knife, slit a large pocket in each steak and fill with 60g (2 oz) of the dolcelatte. Press the steaks back into shape, brush with a little oil and season well. Preheat a heavy-based frying pan until very hot, add the steaks and press down onto the hot surface to seal the steaks quickly. Turn to seal the second side, then continue to cook until the steaks are to your liking. When cooked, remove the steaks to a warm serving plate. Allow the meat juices to reduce a little, then add the port and cream. Continue to cook until the sauce thickens slightly and season. Then pour over the steaks and garnish with watercress.

ROAST PORK WITH FRUITY STUFFING

Preparation time:	Serves:	Total cooking time:
10 minutes	4	1 hour 45 mins

1 kg (2.2 lb) loin pork, boned and skin scored

Oil and salt

1 pear, peeled, cored and chopped

Rind of half a lemon and 5ml (1 tsp) lemon juice

110g (4 oz) ready to eat prunes, chopped

40g (1½ oz) breadcrumbs

Salt and freshly ground black pepper

1 egg

Place the pork, skin side up, in a colander and pour boiling water over the joint. Pat dry and rub generously with oil and salt to give a crisp crackling. Mix all the remaining ingredients together in a bowl and use to stuff the loin of pork. Tie with string at intervals to hold the stuffing in place and ensure that the joint retains its shape. Set up the deep roasting tray, place the joint skin side up on the wire rack, and roast until well cooked and crisp. Cover with foil and leave to rest in a warm place for 10 minutes before carving. Remove the crackling and break into pieces. Serve the pork in slices with the stuffing and a little crackling, accompanied by roast potatoes and seasonal vegetables.

Function	Cooking time	Preheating	Shelf position
Auto roast 185°C	1 hour 45 mins	No	First

Time: 30 minutes per 450g (1lb) plus 35 minutes or use the roast probe: 80 – 85°C

SUGAR-GLAZED BAKED GAMMON

Preparation time:	Serves:	Total cooking time:
5 minutes	10	3 hrs –3 hrs 30 mins

4.5kg (10 lb) ham on the bone

6 peppercorns

1 bayleaf

10 – 15 cloves

60ml (4 tbsp) demerara sugar

2 oranges, sliced

1 small onion, thinly sliced

Black olives, pitted

Place the ham in a large pan with the peppercorns and bayleaf. Cover with cold water and slowly bring to the boil, skimming off any scum that forms. Calculate the total cooking time at 15 minutes per 450g (1 lb) + 20 minutes, and simmer, covered, for half of this time, approximately 1½ hours for a 4.5kg (10 lb) joint. Remove from the pan and allow to cool slightly. Cut off the rind and score the fat in a diamond pattern using a sharp knife. Wrap the meat in foil and place on the deep roasting tray. Bake in the oven at 180°C for 1 hour. Remove the meat from the oven and raise the temperature to 220°C. Stud the diamond shapes with cloves and sprinkle the surface with sugar, patting it in. Cover again with the foil and bake for the remaining cooking time, unwrapping the foil towards the end to allow the fat to crisp. Transfer to a warm serving plate and garnish with orange slices, thinly sliced onion and black olives.

Function	Cooking time	Preheating	Shelf position
Fan heat180°+220°C	1 hr + 30 mins	Yes	First

ROAST PORK WITH FRUITY STUFFING

SUGAR-GLAZED BAKED GAMMON

SWEET & SOUR PORK

Preparation time:	Serves:	Total cooking time:
15 minutes	4	20 minutes

45ml (3 tbsp) groundnut oil

15ml (3 tbsp) sesame seed oil

350g (12 oz) pork fillet strips

1 onion, finely chopped and 1 clove garlic, crushed

5ml (1 tsp) Chinese five spice powder

1 carrot, cut into julienne strips

60g (2½ oz) water chestnuts, sliced

Half a red pepper and half a green pepper, sliced

110g (4 oz) baby sweetcorn

45ml (3 tbsp) dark soy sauce

2 tomatoes, cut into wedges and 110g (4 oz) beansprouts

15ml (1 tbsp) soft brown sugar and 10ml (2 tsp) cornflour

225g (8 oz) tin pineapple chunks in juice

15ml (1 tbsp) white wine vinegar

Salt and freshly ground black pepper

Put the oils into a wok or large frying pan and heat until hot. Add the pork, onion, garlic and five spice powder, and stir fry for 5 minutes. Stir in the carrot, water chestnuts, peppers and sweetcorn, and fry for 3 minutes. Add the soy sauce and cook for a further 2 minutes, stirring continuously. Add the tomatoes, beansprouts and sugar, and fry for 2 minutes. Mix the cornflour to a paste with a little pineapple juice and stir into the wok, together with the remaining ingredients. Bring to the boil and cook for 2–3 minutes until the sauce has thickened and the meat and vegetables are cooked to taste. Serve immediately with boiled rice.

PORK IN APPLE & SULTANA SAUCE

Preparation time:	Serves:	Total cooking time:
10 minutes	4	1 hour

450g (1 lb) pork tenderloin, sliced

Seasoned flour

30ml (2 tbsp) olive oil

1 large onion, chopped

350ml (12 fl oz) dry cider

25g (1 oz) sultanas

Large pinch of dried sage

1 crisp eating apple, thickly sliced

Salt and freshly ground black pepper

45ml (3 tbsp) crème fraîche or double cream

Toss the pork slices in the seasoned flour. Heat the oil in a flameproof casserole and sauté the onion until soft, then add the meat and seal quickly. Mix in the cider, sultanas, sage, apple and seasoning. Bring to the boil, then transfer the casserole dish to the oven and cook for 40–50 minutes. Stir in the crème fraîche or double cream, then strain the sauce into a saucepan, retaining the meat in the covered casserole dish to keep warm. Reduce the sauce on the hob for a few minutes, then add the meat to the pan and reheat gently. Serve with sautéed potatoes and roasted root vegetables (page 95).

Function	Cooking time	Preheating	Shelf position
Fan heat 200ºC	40 – 50 minutes	No	First

BRAISED PORK WITH PLUMS & GINGER

Preparation time:	Serves:	Total cooking time:
10 minutes	4	40 – 45 minutes

450g (1 lb) plums, stoned and diced

2.5cm (1 inch) piece ginger, grated

Salt and freshly ground black pepper

15ml (1 tbsp) olive oil

5ml (1 tsp) sesame seed oil

4 pork chops, approximately 200g (7 oz) each

2.5ml (½ tsp) Chinese five spice powder

60ml (4 tbsp) white wine

10cm (4 inch) strip orange peel

3 sprigs fresh thyme

175ml (6 fl oz) vegetable stock

Spread the plums and ginger over the base of a lightly greased ovenproof dish. Season with salt and pepper and bake in the oven for 20 minutes. Meanwhile, heat the oils in a frying pan, add the pork chops and five spice powder, and fry on both sides until browned. Remove with a slotted spoon and arrange on top of the plums. Add the wine to the frying pan and scrape the base to loosen any sediment. Pour over the pork. Tuck the orange peel and thyme under the pork and add the stock. Bake in the oven for 20 – 25 minutes until the pork is cooked. Serve with stir-fried vegetables, flavoured with a little of the sauce.

Function	Cooking time	Preheating	Shelf position
Fan heat 200°C	20 + 20 – 25 mins	No	First

CROWN ROAST OF LAMB

Preparation time:	Serves:	Total cooking time:
15 minutes	4 – 6	1hr 30 – 1 hr 45 mins

2 pieces best end neck (6 cutlets each)
trimmed and prepared for roasting – approx 1.4kg (3 lb)

Half an onion, finely chopped

110g (4 oz) fresh breadcrumbs

1 clove garlic, crushed

110g (4 oz) lamb trimmings, minced (optional)

Half a stick celery, finely chopped

10ml (2 tsp) fresh rosemary, chopped

10ml (2 tsp) fresh mint, chopped

1 egg, beaten

Salt and freshly ground black pepper

Set up the deep roasting tray and place the prepared crown on the wire rack. Mix all the remaining ingredients together in a bowl and fill the crown with the stuffing. Twist small pieces of foil around the tops of the exposed bones to prevent them burning. Cover the stuffing with a circle of foil to prevent burning and roast for 1 hour 30 mins to 1 hour 45 mins according to taste. Remove the circle of foil 15 minutes before the end of the cooking time to brown and crisp the stuffing. Variation: Leave the centre unstuffed (fill with foil so that it retains its shape). Reduce the cooking time by approximately 10 minutes. Just before serving fill with vegetables such as a small cauliflower or new potatoes garnished with parsley butter.

Function	Cooking time	Preheating	Shelf position
Auto roast 170°C	1 hr 30 – 45 mins	No	First

ROAST LAMB
WITH SPICY RED PEPPER CRUST

Preparation time:	Serves:	Total cooking time:
15 minutes + chilling	4	1 hour 15 – 30 mins

15ml (1 tbsp) olive oil and half a red pepper, finely diced

275g (10 oz) fine breadcrumbs

150g (5 oz) butter, softened

1 large clove garlic, crushed

30ml (2 tbsp) ground medium hot chilli powder

Pinch of sea salt

1 kg (2¼ lb) lean shoulder of lamb

Salt and freshly ground black pepper

Heat the oil in a saucepan. Sauté the red pepper for 3 minutes. Remove from the heat and stir in the breadcrumbs, butter, garlic, chilli powder and salt. Mix until well combined. Spread the mixture onto a baking tray to form a crust large enough to coat the lamb. Use the flat of the hand to level the mixture. Chill in the refrigerator for about 30 minutes or until firm. Meanwhile, generously season the lamb with salt and pepper. Set up the deep roasting tray and place the lamb on the wire rack. Roast, uncovered, for approximately 40 minutes, allowing 15–20 minutes per 450g (1 lb). This timing will give a slightly pink result. Add a further 10 minutes if you prefer the meat well done. Remove the lamb from the oven, season again and cover with aluminium foil. Turn off the oven. Replace the lamb in the oven and let it continue cooking in the residual heat for 20 minutes. The meat can be prepared to this stage earlier in the day, as it is going to be reheated just before serving. Approximately 20 minutes before serving time, preheat the oven using the fan grill at 220°C. Remove the foil from the lamb and cover the surface of the meat in the prepared breadcrumb mixture, pressing firmly. Place the lamb in the oven and finish cooking on the fan grill setting for about 10 minutes until the crust is golden brown and the lamb has heated through thoroughly.

Function	Cooking time	Preheating	Shelf position
Auto roast 200°C	40 – 50 minutes	No	First

Function	Cooking time	Preheating	Shelf position
Fan grill 220°C	10 minutes	Yes	Third

ROAST LAMB
WITH GARLIC & ROSEMARY

Preparation time:	Serves:	Total cooking time:
5 minutes	4	1 hour 35 – 45 mins

1kg (2¼ lb) leg of lamb

2 cloves garlic, sliced and fresh rosemary

Salt and freshly ground pepper

Pierce the lamb with a sharp knife and insert slivers of garlic and rosemary into the cuts. Season with salt and pepper. Set up the deep roasting tray and place the lamb in the centre of the wire rack. Roast in the oven, basting occasionally. When cooked, cover with foil and leave to rest in a warm place for 15 minutes before carving. Serve with mint sauce or redcurrant jelly, new potatoes and green vegetables. NB: for meat off the bone, add about 15 minutes to the total cooking time.

Function	Cooking time	Preheating	Shelf position
Auto roast 180°C	1 hr 35 – 45 mins	No	First

Time: 25 minutes per 450g (1 lb) plus 30 minutes, or use the Roast probe: 75 – 80°C

FESTIVE LAMB & COCONUT CURRY

Preparation time:	Serves:	Total cooking time:
15 minutes	4	2 hours

60ml (4 tbsp) vegetable oil

3 green cardamom pods and 4 cloves

2.5 cm (1 inch) cinnamon stick

30ml (2 tbsp) garam masala

2.5 cm (1 inch) fresh ginger, grated

1 large red onion, sliced

450g (1 lb) lean lamb, cubed

3 potatoes, peeled and cut into 2.5 cm (1 inch) cubes

2 carrots, chopped and 5ml (1 tsp) salt

2 fresh red chillies, finely chopped

150ml (¼ pint) coconut milk

60ml (4 tbsp) fresh coriander leaves, chopped

Heat the oil in a large frying pan. Fry the cardamom pods, cloves, cinnamon and garam masala for 30 seconds, stirring continuously – do not allow to burn. Mix in the ginger and onion. Stir fry for 4 minutes to soften the onion. Add the lamb cubes and fry for 10 minutes until the meat is well browned. Stir in the potatoes, carrots, salt, chillies and 570ml (1 pint) of water. Cover and bring to the boil. Turn into a casserole dish and cook in the oven until the meat is very tender and the sauce has thickened. Mash a few of the potatoes to help thicken the sauce if necessary. Stir in the coconut milk and the coriander leaves just before serving with basmati rice.

Function	Cooking time	Preheating	Shelf position
Fan heat 180°C	1 hour 45 mins	No	First

GALWAY LAMB BAKE

Preparation time:	Serves:	Total cooking time:
15 minutes	4	45 minutes

450g (1 lb) lamb neck fillet, diced

Salt and freshly ground black pepper

30ml (2 tbsp) plain flour

40g (1½ oz) unsalted butter and 1 large onion, sliced

350ml (12 fl oz) lamb or beef stock

3 tomatoes, skinned and chopped

1 bayleaf and 2 sprigs fresh thyme

15ml (1 tbsp) Worcester sauce

1kg (2¼ lb) potatoes, peeled and quartered

75ml (3 fl oz) whole milk

1 bunch spring onions, chopped

Toss the diced lamb in seasoned flour. Heat half the butter in a large frying pan and sauté the lamb until browned. Add the onion and cook until softened. Pour in the stock, scraping any sediment from the bottom of the pan. Add the tomatoes, bayleaf, thyme and the Worcester sauce. Bring to the boil, reduce the heat and simmer uncovered until the sauce has reduced by one third and thickened slightly. Meanwhile, boil and mash the potatoes. Mix the milk, remaining butter and spring onions together in a saucepan. Bring slowly to the boil, and pour into the mashed potatoes. Mix well and season. Spoon the lamb and the reduced sauce into a large casserole dish. Pipe or spoon the potatoes over the lamb, ensuring the meat is completely covered. Bake in the oven until the topping is crisp. Serve with cabbage and roasted root vegetables (see page 95).

Function	Cooking time	Preheating	Shelf position
Fan grill 190°C	25 minutes	No	Second

SAVOURY SUPPERS

TWO-CHEESE ITALIAN FLAN

Preparation time:	Serves:	Total cooking time:
10 minutes + chilling	4 – 6	25 minutes

Pastry	175g (6 oz) plain flour and a pinch of salt
	75g (3 oz) butter
	1 egg
	30 – 45ml (2 – 3 tbsp) water
Filling	110g (4 oz) toasted pine nuts
	50g (2 oz) sun-dried tomatoes
	40g (1½ oz) black olives
	2.5ml (½ tsp) garlic purée
	60ml (4 tbsp) fresh basil
	150g (5 oz) Provolone medium hard Italian cheese, grated
	250g (9 oz) mascarpone cheese
	2 eggs
	30ml (2 tbsp) single cream

For the pastry, mix together the flour and salt in a bowl. Rub in the butter until the mixture resembles fine breadcrumbs. Mix in the egg and enough water to give a firm dough. Wrap in clingfilm and place in the refrigerator for 30 minutes. Roll out the pastry on a lightly floured surface and use to line a lightly greased 25cm (10 inch) flan dish. Leave to chill in the refrigerator. In an electric blender, lightly process the pine nuts, sun-dried tomatoes, olives, garlic purée and basil to form a rough paste. Spread the paste over the base of the pastry case. Beat the remaining ingredients together and pour over the paste. Bake until golden brown and firm to the touch.

Function	Cooking time	Preheating	Shelf position
Int. bake 200°C	25 minutes	No	First

HERB SAUSAGES WITH CARAMELIZED ONIONS

Preparation time:	Serves:	Total cooking time:
10 minutes	4	40 minutes

25g (1 oz) butter
30ml (2 tbsp) olive oil
350g (12 oz) button onions, peeled
30ml (2 tbsp) caster sugar
Salt and freshly ground black pepper
450g (1 lb) quality pork sausages or sausagemeat
30ml (2 tbsp) mixed fresh herbs (thyme, chives, oregano)
15ml (1 tbsp) wholegrain mustard
10ml (2 tsp) Worcester sauce

Heat the butter and oil in a frying pan, and add the onions and sugar. Stir well, season, cover with a lid and cook on a low heat for about 20 minutes until the onions are just tender. Shake the pan occasionally, but do not lift the lid too often or the onions will stick. Meanwhile, remove the skins from the sausages and mix the meat with the herbs, mustard and Worcester sauce. Shape into 12 small, flat rounds. Place on the deep roasting tray and grill until they are cooked through, turning over once. Serve the sausages with the caramelized onions and sautéed potatoes.

Function	Cooking time	Preheating	Shelf position
Grill 200°C	13–15 minutes	No	Fourth

PIZZAS

Preparation time:	Makes:	Total cooking time:
20 minutes + proving	2 medium bases	35 minutes

Base	450g (1 lb) strong plain flour
	5ml (1 tsp) salt
	50g (2 oz) butter, softened
	1 sachet easy blend dried yeast
	150ml (5 fl oz) tepid milk
Sauce	30ml (2 tbsp) extra virgin olive oil
	1 onion, chopped
	1 clove garlic, finely chopped
	275ml (½ pint) passata sauce
	4 sprigs fresh thyme
	45ml (3 tbsp) fresh parsley, chopped
	Salt and freshly ground black pepper

In a bowl, mix together the flour, salt and butter until the mixture resembles fine breadcrumbs. Stir in the yeast. Slowly add the tepid milk to the flour mixture and blend, adding more milk as necessary, until the dough forms a ball. Turn the dough onto a floured surface and knead well for 10 minutes. Place the dough in a bowl and cover with a cloth. Leave to rise in the oven set on fan heat at 40°C for about 40 minutes, until the dough has doubled in size. Tip the dough out onto a floured surface and cut it into 2 pieces. Roll out each piece until it is the size of a large dinner plate. Place on 2 lightly oiled baking trays dusted with flour. Cover and leave to rise again in the oven, set on fan heat at 40°C, for a further 20 minutes.

To make the base sauce, heat the olive oil in a saucepan and fry the onion until soft and translucent. Add the garlic and cook for a further 1 minute. Stir in the passata sauce, herbs and seasoning. Bring to the boil, reduce the heat and simmer, uncovered, until the sauce has reduced by a third. Spread the tomato sauce over the 2 pizza dough bases, leaving a 2cm (¾ inch) rim clear round the edge. Choose two of the toppings given, and arrange the ingredients on top of the sauce. Drizzle the extra virgin olive oil over the pizzas and bake in the oven. Cut into portions and serve with a mixed green leaf salad.

SPICY SAUSAGE TOPPING

Covers one pizza base

5 slices chorizo sausage
Half a red pepper, blanched and finely sliced
1 large tomato, sliced
125g (4½ oz) buffalo mozzarella, sliced
8 pitted black olives
30ml (2 tbsp) extra virgin olive oil

QUATTRO FORMAGGI TOPPING

Covers one pizza base

50g (2 oz) Gorgonzola, crumbled
50g (2 oz) mozzarella, sliced
50g (2 oz) Gruyère, grated
50g (2 oz) Bel Paese, grated
Fresh basil leaves
Black olives, pitted (optional)
30ml (2 tbsp) extra virgin olive oil
Freshly ground black pepper

WILD MUSHROOM TOPPING

Covers one pizza base

125g (4¹/₂ oz) buffalo mozzarella, sliced

3 shallots, peeled and sliced

40g (1¹/₂ oz) chanterelle mushrooms, sliced

50g (2 oz) chestnut mushrooms, sliced

Few sprigs fresh oregano and snipped chives

30ml (2 tbsp) extra virgin olive oil

Salt and freshly ground black pepper

PESCATORE TOPPING

Covers one pizza base

50g (2 oz) flaked tuna

25 – 50g (1 – 2 oz) peeled prawns

25g (1 oz) bottled mussels, drained

125g (4¹/₂ oz) buffalo mozzarella, sliced

Half a green pepper, blanched and finely sliced

25g (1 oz) sweetcorn kernels

15ml (1 tbsp) fresh dill, finely chopped

30ml (2 tbsp) extra virgin olive oil

Function	Cooking time	Preheating	Shelf position
Int. bake 190ºC	20 minutes	No	First

SPANISH OMELETTE

Preparation time:	Serves:	Total cooking time:
15 minutes	4	25 minutes

30ml (2 tbsp) olive oil

1 onion, chopped

3 rashers bacon, chopped

Half a red pepper, chopped

3 mushrooms, sliced

40g (1¹/₂ oz) peas

2 cooked potatoes, diced

4 large eggs

Salt and freshly ground black pepper

30ml (2 tbsp) fresh parsley, chopped

Heat the oil in a frying pan. Add the onion, bacon and red pepper and fry until the vegetables are soft but not coloured. Stir in the mushrooms and peas, and cook for a further 1–2 minutes. Add the potatoes and heat through. Beat the eggs with the salt and pepper and pour over the vegetables. Cook the base of the omelette over a medium heat, covered with a lid. When the underneath is just set, transfer the pan to the oven and grill the top of the omelette until set. Serve immediately with crusty bread and a mixed green salad.

Function	Cooking time	Preheating	Shelf position
Grill 240ºC	3 –5 minutes	Yes	Fourth

PIZZA WITH SPICY SAUSAGE TOPPING

STILTON & BACON QUICHE
(LARGE PARTY QUANTITY)

Preparation time:	Serves:	Total cooking time:
15 minutes + chilling	20	30 – 40 minutes

Pastry	450g (1 lb) plain flour
	5ml (1 tsp) salt
	225g (8oz) butter
	150ml (5 fl oz) water
Filling	225g (8 oz) crumbled Lancashire cheese
	225g (8 oz) crumbled Stilton cheese
	12 rashers smoked streaky bacon, cooked and chopped
	9 eggs
	425ml (¾ pint) single cream
	425ml (¾ pint) milk
	Salt and freshly ground black pepper

For the pastry, mix together the flour and salt in a bowl. Rub in the butter until the mixture resembles fine breadcrumbs. Mix in enough water to give a firm dough. Wrap in clingfilm and place in the refrigerator for 30 minutes. Roll out the pastry on a lightly floured surface. Lightly grease the Miele deep roasting tray and line with the pastry. Sprinkle the cheese and bacon over the pastry. Whisk the eggs with the cream and milk and add the seasoning. Pour the mixture over the cheese and bacon, and season with freshly ground black pepper. Bake until the quiche is golden brown and just set.

Function	Cooking time	Preheating	Shelf position
Int. bake 180°C	30 –40 minutes	No	First

PIQUANT CAULIFLOWER & BACON AU GRATIN

Preparation time:	Serves:	Total cooking time:
10 minutes	4	20 minutes

1 cauliflower, quartered

Salt

40g (1½ oz) butter

1 onion, chopped

45ml (3 tbsp) plain flour

15ml (1 tbsp) mustard powder

5ml (1 tsp) hot paprika

425ml (¾ pint) milk

50g (2oz) mature Cheddar, grated

3 rashers smoked bacon, cooked and chopped

Cook the cauliflower in plenty of salted boiling water until al dente. Drain and place in an ovenproof casserole dish. In another saucepan, melt the butter and fry the onion until soft. Stir in the flour, mustard and half the paprika. Cook for 1–2 minutes. Gradually stir in the milk and cook until the sauce thickens, stirring continuously. Remove from the heat and add the cheese. Pour the cheese sauce over the cauliflower. Arrange the pieces of bacon on top, and sprinkle with the remaining paprika. Place under the preheated grill until the bacon is crisp and the sauce is golden and bubbling gently.

Function	Cooking time	Preheating	Shelf position
Fan grill 250°C	6 – 8 minutes	Yes	Third

ITALIAN KEBABS

Preparation time:	Serves:	Total cooking time:
20 minutes + marinading	4	15 minutes

4 x 75g (3 oz) slices of veal

4 slices of smoked ham

30 basil leaves

60ml (4 tbsp) olive oil

30ml (2 tbsp) white wine vinegar

Salt and freshly ground black pepper

Beat out the veal with a rolling pin until even in thickness and flat. Cut each piece into 4 strips. Cut each slice of ham into 4 strips. Place a strip of ham over a strip of veal. Add a basil leaf and roll up like a Catherine wheel. Place in a shallow dish. Mix together the oil and vinegar. Tear the remaining basil leaves and stir into the marinade. Season with a little salt and plenty of freshly ground black pepper. Pour over the veal rolls. Cover and leave in the refrigerator to marinate for at least 2 hours, preferably overnight. Thread the rolls onto skewers. Cook the kebabs under a moderately hot grill for about 15 minutes, turning frequently, and baste occasionally with the marinade. Serve with herb rice and roasted vegetables or a salad and crusty bread.

Function	Cooking time	Preheating	Shelf position
Fan grill 200°C	15 minutes	Yes	Fourth

HAM & BEAN CASSEROLE

Preparation time:	Serves:	Total cooking time:
15 minutes	4 – 6	1 hour

15ml (1 tbsp) olive oil

2 onions, chopped

1 clove garlic, finely chopped

2 cloves

450g (1 lb) piece cooked ham or hock, cubed

2 sprigs fresh thyme

Pinch of dried marjoram

150ml (5 fl oz) passata sauce

275ml (½ pint) ham or chicken stock

450g (1 lb) potatoes, peeled and parboiled

400g (14 oz) tin cannellini beans, drained

Freshly ground black pepper

30ml (2 tbsp) fresh parsley, chopped

Heat the oil in a large, flameproof casserole dish. Sauté the onions until soft and translucent. Add the garlic and cloves and cook gently for 1 minute. Stir in the ham, herbs, passata and stock. Bring to the boil. Chop the parboiled potatoes and add to the casserole. Season with plenty of black pepper. Cover and cook in the oven for 30 minutes. Add the cannellini beans and cook for a further 10 minutes, or until the potatoes are soft and beginning to break down and thicken the casserole. Sprinkle with chopped parsley and serve with hot, crusty bread.

Function	Cooking time	Preheating	Shelf position
Fan heat 190°C	40 minutes	No	First

H A M   &   B E A N   C A S S E R O L E

MIELE QUICHE LORRAINE

Preparation time:	Serves:	Total cooking time:
15 minutes + chilling	4 – 6	35 minutes

Pastry	175g (6 oz) plain flour
	Pinch of salt
	75g (3 oz) butter
	1 egg
	30 – 45ml (2 – 3 tbsp) water
Filling	6 rashers smoked bacon, chopped
	1 large onion, chopped
	1 leek, sliced
	50g (2 oz) mushrooms, sliced
	1 tomato, seeded and chopped (optional)
	110g (4 oz) mature Cheddar, grated
	Half a green pepper, sliced
	2 eggs
	150ml (¼ pint) single cream
	150ml (¼ pint) milk
	Salt and pepper

For the pastry, mix together the flour and salt in a bowl. Rub in the butter until the mixture resembles fine bread-crumbs. Mix in the egg and enough water to give a firm dough. Wrap in clingfilm and place in the refrigerator for 30 minutes. Roll out the pastry on a lightly floured surface and line a lightly greased 25cm (10 inch) flan dish. Leave to chill in the refrigerator. For the filling, lightly fry the bacon, onion and leek in a pan until soft and just cooked. Drain off any excess liquid and place in the pastry case with the mushrooms, tomato (if using), and pepper.

Cover the surface of the quiche with the cheese. Beat the eggs, cream and milk together, season and pour over the filling. Bake until the quiche is golden brown and just set.

Function	Cooking time	Preheating	Shelf position
Int. bake 190ºC	30 minutes	No	First

TOAD IN THE HOLE

Preparation time:	Serves:	Total cooking time:
5 minutes + standing	4	50 minutes

110g (4 oz) plain flour
Pinch of salt
2 eggs
275ml (½ pint) milk
15ml (1 tbsp) vegetable oil
8 pork sausages, pierced

Place the flour and salt in a bowl and make a well in the centre. Gradually add the eggs, then the milk, and whisk until smooth. Leave the batter to stand for 30 minutes. Pour the oil into a deep-sided ovenproof dish. Place in the oven until the oil is very hot. Add the sausages and bake for 10 minutes in the oil, turning halfway through cooking. Pour in the batter and cook until the batter is well risen, golden brown and just set in the middle. Serve immediately with onion gravy.

Function	Cooking time	Preheating	Shelf position
Fan heat 200ºC	40 minutes	No	First

LEEK & BACON QUICHE

STUFFED PEPPERS

VEGETARIAN DISHES

QUORN & LEEK PIE

Preparation time:	Serves:	Total cooking time:
10 minutes + infusing	4	1 hour

300ml (11 fl oz) milk

1 small onion and a small piece of carrot, chopped

1 stick celery, chopped

1 bayleaf and 3 peppercorns

25g (1 oz) butter and 45ml (3 tbsp) plain flour

30ml (2 tbsp) olive oil

3 large leeks, sliced

350g (12 oz) Quorn pieces (or cooked chicken)

50g (2 oz) mature Cheddar, grated

Salt and freshly ground black pepper

350g (12 oz) puff pastry and 1 egg, beaten

Make a béchamel sauce by putting the milk, onion, carrot, celery, bayleaf and peppercorns in a saucepan and slowly bring to the boil. Remove from the heat, cover and leave to infuse for 15 minutes. Strain the liquid and discard the vegetables. Melt the butter in a clean saucepan and stir in the flour. Cook for 1 minute, then gradually add the milk, stirring continuously until the sauce thickens and is smooth. Remove the sauce from the heat and reserve. Heat the oil in a medium saucepan. Sauté the leeks and Quorn (or chicken) together until the leeks have softened. Stir in the béchamel sauce and remove from the heat. Add the grated cheese and season to taste. Spoon the mixture into a suitable pie dish. Roll out the pastry and use to cover the pie dish. Glaze with the beaten egg and bake until the pastry is golden brown.

Function	Cooking time	Preheating	Shelf position
Fan heat 180°C	30 – 35 minutes	No	First

STUFFED PEPPERS

Preparation time:	Serves:	Total cooking time:
15 minutes	4	45 minutes

4 medium red peppers

110g (4 oz) long grain rice

1.2 litres (2 pints) vegetable stock

50g (2 oz) sunflower seeds

1 bunch spring onions, chopped

2 tomatoes, skinned and chopped

60ml (4 tbsp) sweetcorn kernels

60ml (4 tbsp) fresh parsley, chopped

30ml (2 tbsp) sultanas

Salt and freshly ground black pepper

60ml (4 tbsp) extra virgin olive oil (optional)

Cut a cap off the tops of the peppers and remove the seeds. Blanch in boiling salted water. Boil the rice in the vegetable stock until just cooked. Drain well and put the rice into a mixing bowl. Stir in the remaining ingredients, mixing well. Fill the peppers with the rice mixture and top with the caps. Place the peppers on a baking tray and cook until they are soft and just beginning to colour. Serve hot or warm, drizzled with extra virgin olive oil if desired.

Function	Cooking time	Preheating	Shelf position
Fan heat 195°C	25 minutes	No	First

SAVOURY STRUDEL

Preparation time:	Serves:	Total cooking time:
30 minutes	6	40 minutes

150g (5 oz) unsalted butter

30ml (2 tbsp) olive oil

450g (1 lb) potatoes, peeled and diced

450g (1 lb) carrots, diced

225g (8 oz) leeks, sliced

1 bunch spring onions, chopped

450g (1 lb) spring greens, shredded

1 clove garlic, crushed

15ml (1 tbsp) lemon juice

275ml (½ pint) fromage frais

Ground mixed spice

Salt and freshly ground black pepper

Pinch of paprika

4 large sheets of filo pastry

75g (3 oz) ground almonds

5ml (1 tsp) poppy or sesame seeds

Melt 50g (2 oz) butter with half the oil in a large frying pan. Add the potatoes, carrots, leeks and spring onions, and sauté for 5 minutes. Add 110ml (4 fl oz) boiling water, cover and simmer for 15 minutes. Leave to cool. Meanwhile, melt 25g (1 oz) butter with the remaining oil, and sauté the spring greens and garlic for 2 minutes until just wilted. Stir in the lemon juice and cool. Stir the fromage frais into the potato mixture and season with mixed spice, salt, pepper and paprika. Melt the remaining butter and brush one sheet of filo pastry. Overlap with a second sheet to make a 45cm (18 inch) square. Brush with melted butter.

Repeat the process with the remaining pastry to make a double thickness. Sprinkle the ground almonds over the pastry. Spoon the potato mixture over the pastry, leaving a border at the edge, and top with the spring greens. Fold the sides over the filling and roll up. Brush with butter and sprinkle with the seeds. Bake until the pastry is crisp and golden.

Function	Cooking time	Preheating	Shelf position
Fan heat 190ºC	25 minutes	Yes	First

WINTER STEW WITH HERB DUMPLINGS

Preparation time:	Serves:	Total cooking time:
20 minutes	4	45 minutes

45ml (3 tbsp) olive oil

350g (12 oz) shallots, peeled

1 clove garlic, crushed

2 sticks celery, sliced

2 carrots, cut into batons

2 large parsnips, sliced

225g (8 oz) pumpkin flesh, cubed

15ml (1 tbsp) plain flour

30ml (2 tbsp) fresh parsley, chopped

275ml (½ pint) vegetable stock

275ml (½ pint) dark stout

30ml (2 tbsp) Worcester sauce

2 bayleaves and 1 fresh bouquet garni

30ml (2 tbsp) tomato purée

Salt and freshly ground black pepper

100g (3½ oz) self-raising flour and some salt

40g (1½ oz) vegetable suet

60ml (4 tbsp) fresh mixed herbs, chopped

60ml (4 tbsp) milk

Heat the oil in a large flameproof casserole. Sauté the shallots, garlic and celery until golden. Add the remaining vegetables and sauté until lightly browned. Sprinkle with plain flour and stir in. Add the fresh parsley, stock, stout, Worcester sauce, bayleaves, bouquet garni, tomato purée and seasoning. Bring to the boil, cover and bake in the oven for 20 minutes.

Meanwhile, to make the dumplings, mix the self-raising flour, salt, suet and herbs together in a bowl. Stir in the milk, binding to a firm dough. Using floured hands, roll the mixture into 12 small dumplings. Remove the casserole from the oven and stir well. Arrange the dumplings on the surface. Return to the oven, uncovered, for a further 20 minutes, cooking until the dumplings are light and fluffy. Serve immediately.

Function	Cooking time	Preheating	Shelf position
Fan heat 180°C	40 minutes	No	First

HONEY-GLAZED VEGETABLE TARTE TATIN

Preparation time:	Serves:	Total cooking time:
15 minutes + chilling	4	45 minutes

175g (6 oz) plain flour

2.5ml (½ tsp) salt

5ml (1 tsp) mustard powder

75g (3 oz) butter

25g (1 oz) Parmesan cheese, grated

45ml (3 tbsp) olive oil

350g (12 oz) parsnips, thickly sliced

100g (3½ oz) baby onions, thickly sliced

1 potato, parboiled and quartered

30ml (2 tbsp) clear honey

15ml (1 tbsp) raspberry or red wine vinegar

Salt and freshly ground black pepper

Sift the flour, salt and mustard powder into a bowl. Rub in the butter until the mixture resembles fine breadcrumbs, and stir in the Parmesan. Sprinkle on 30–45ml (2–3 tbsp) iced water and mix to a firm dough. Cover with clingfilm and chill for 30 minutes. Put the oil in a 25cm (9 inch) round gratin dish. Heat in the oven for 10 minutes until hot. Arrange the vegetables in a single layer in the dish and drizzle over the honey and vinegar. Season well. Bake in the oven for about 15 minutes or until the vegetables are golden underneath and just cooked. Do not turn or disturb the vegetable layer.

Roll out the pastry to the same diameter as the dish. Place on top of the vegetables and press down round the edges so that it fits snugly. Bake for 20 minutes until the pastry is cooked and golden brown. Remove from the oven and leave to stand for about 5 minutes. Invert onto a serving plate, so that the vegetables are on top, and season well. Serve warm with tomato coulis (see page 140).

Function	Cooking time	Preheating	Shelf position
Fan heat 200°C	45 minutes	No	First

RATATOUILLE WITH MOZZARELLA

Preparation time:	Serves:	Total cooking time:
20 minutes + draining	4	45 minutes

125g (4½ oz) aubergine and some salt

1 green pepper

1 red pepper

200g (7 oz) courgettes

110ml (4 fl oz) olive oil

1 onion, chopped

1 clove garlic, crushed

4 plum tomatoes, peeled

1 bayleaf, 1 sprig thyme and a few sprigs parsley

Freshly ground black pepper

75g (3 oz) mozzarella cheese

30ml (2 tbsp) extra virgin olive oil

Cut the aubergine into slices. Put them in a colander and sprinkle with salt, then leave to drain for 30 minutes. Chop the peppers and courgettes into similar sized pieces. Heat half the olive oil in a frying pan and cook the onion and garlic until soft and translucent. Using a slotted spoon, transfer the onion and garlic to a heatproof casserole dish. Repeat the process with the courgettes and peppers. Rinse the sliced aubergine and dry well with kitchen paper. Turn up the heat under the frying pan until the oil is quite hot and sear the aubergine slices for 2 minutes, before transferring to the casserole. Add the tomatoes, herbs and remaining oil, and season with salt and plenty of freshly ground black pepper. Top with thin slices of the mozzarella, and cover with a tight-fitting lid. Cook in the oven until the vegetables are soft and the tomatoes have broken down. Just before serving, drizzle the 30ml (2 tbsp) of extra virgin olive oil over the top of the cheese.

Function	Cooking time	Preheating	Shelf position
Fan heat 190ºC	30 minutes	No	First

CHEESE & NUT ROAST

Preparation time:	Serves:	Total cooking time:
15 minutes	4 – 6	1 hour 40 minutes

1 red pepper, halved and deseeded

50g (2 oz) unsalted butter

2 onions and 1 clove garlic, finely chopped

75g (3 oz) wholemeal breadcrumbs

225g (8 oz) brazil nuts, chopped

225g (8 oz) mature Cheddar cheese, grated

1 egg, lightly beaten, and a good pinch of cayenne pepper

Salt and freshly ground black pepper

Grease and base line a 900g (2 lb) loaf tin. Remove the white parts from the red pepper, and grill with the skin uppermost until the skin starts to blacken and shrivel. Cool slightly and skin. Dice the pepper and reserve. Melt the butter in a large saucepan and sauté the onion and garlic until soft and golden. Remove from the heat and add all the other ingredients, mixing well. Spoon the mixture into the prepared tin, packing down well. Bake in the oven until the top is crisp and golden brown. Serve in slices with warm tomato coulis or stroganoff sauce (both on page 140).

Function	Cooking time	Preheating	Shelf position
Fan heat 185ºC	1 hour 30 mins	No	First

RATATOUILLE WITH MOZZARELLA

BUTTERBEAN BIRYANI

Preparation time:	Serves:	Total cooking time:
15 minutes	4	55 minutes

30ml (2 tbsp) olive oil

5ml (1 tsp) poppy seeds and 5ml (1 tsp) mustard seeds

225g (8 oz) long grain brown rice

1.25ml (¼ tsp) hot chilli powder

5ml (1 tsp) each of turmeric, garam masala & ground coriander

1 aubergine, diced

1 red pepper, sliced into strips

400g (14 oz) tin tomatoes

850ml (1½ pints) vegetable stock

15ml (1 tbsp) dark soy sauce

400g (14 oz) tin butter beans, drained

50g (2 oz) creamed coconut, grated

Heat the oil in a large flameproof casserole. Cook the poppy and mustard seeds over a low heat until the seeds start to pop. Add the rice and cook for 3 minutes, stirring continuously. Mix the dry spices together in a small bowl. Add 30ml (2 tbsp) of cold water and mix to a paste. Stir into the rice, together with the aubergine and red pepper. Cook over a low heat for 3–4 minutes. Add the tin of tomatoes, vegetable stock and soy sauce, and bring to the boil. Cover with a tight-fitting lid and transfer to the oven. Bake until the rice is tender and most of the liquid has been absorbed. Five minutes before the end of the cooking time, stir in the butter beans. When cooked, remove from the oven and add the creamed coconut, stirring until melted. Serve with fresh naan bread and tomato salsa (page 140).

Function	Cooking time	Preheating	Shelf position
Fan heat 190ºC	40 minutes	No	First

RED LEICESTER & WATERCRESS ROULADE

Preparation time:	Serves:	Total cooking time:
15 minutes	4 – 6	25 minutes

50g (2 oz) fresh Parmesan, grated

50g (2 oz) unsalted butter

1 onion, finely chopped

150g (5 oz) watercress, finely chopped

45ml (3 tbsp) fromage frais

4 eggs, separated

50g (2 oz) ground almonds

Salt and freshly ground black pepper

15ml (1 tbsp) plain flour

Good pinch of paprika

275ml (½ pint) milk

15ml (1 tbsp) tomato purée

110g (4 oz) Red Leicester cheese, grated

Grease and line a 25cm (10inch) Swiss roll tin with baking parchment. Sprinkle with half the Parmesan. Melt half the butter in a saucepan and fry the onion until soft and translucent. Remove from the heat and stir in the watercress, fromage frais, beaten egg yolks, ground almonds and remaining Parmesan. Season well with salt and pepper. Whisk the egg whites until stiff and lightly fold into the watercress mixture. Spoon onto the prepared tin and bake for approximately 15 minutes or until set. Meanwhile, melt the rest of the butter in a small saucepan and stir in the flour and paprika. Cook for 1 minute. Gradually add the milk and cook, whisking continuously, until the sauce thickens. Stir in the tomato purée. Remove from the heat and add the Red Leicester cheese, stirring until the cheese melts. Cover with clingfilm and allow to cool a little. Turn the roulade out onto greaseproof paper and carefully peel off the lining paper. Spread the cheese filling over the roulade and roll up. Serve immediately with a crisp mixed salad.

Function	Cooking time	Preheating	Shelf position
Fan heat 190°C	15 minutes	No	First

SPINACH & CREAM CHEESE TORTILLAS

Preparation time: 10 minutes + infusing	Serves: 4	Total cooking time: 40 minutes

570ml (1 pint) milk

Few whole peppercorns and 1 bayleaf

Half a carrot and half a celery stick

Few sprigs of parsley

40g (1½ oz) butter

30ml (2 tbsp) plain flour

175g (6 oz) mature Cheddar cheese, grated

350g (12 oz) frozen chopped spinach, thawed

1 bunch spring onions, chopped

350g (12 oz) cream cheese with herbs

1 egg, beaten

2.5ml (½ tsp) grated nutmeg

2.5ml (½ tsp) hot chilli sauce (optional)

Salt and freshly ground black pepper

8 small wheat tortillas

Place the milk, peppercorns, bayleaf, carrot, celery and parsley in a large saucepan, and slowly bring to the boil. Remove from the heat and leave to infuse for 15 minutes. Strain the milk and discard the flavourings. Melt the butter in a separate large saucepan. Stir in the flour and cook for 1–2 minutes. Gradually add the infused milk, stirring continuously, until the sauce thickens. Remove from the heat, and stir in ¾ of the Cheddar, then put to one side. Press the spinach in a sieve to extract any excess liquid, and mix together with the onions, cream cheese, egg, nutmeg, chilli and seasoning. Divide the spinach mixture between the tortillas and roll up. Pour a thin layer of the cheese sauce into the bottom of an ovenproof dish. Lay the tortillas in the sauce and cover completely with the remaining sauce. Sprinkle with the remaining grated cheese and bake in the oven until the top is golden brown. Serve with tomato salsa (see page 140).

Function	Cooking time	Preheating	Shelf position
Fan heat 200°C	30 minutes	No	First

STIR-FRIED GREENS WITH HALLOUMI CHEESE

STIR-FRIED GREENS WITH HALLOUMI CHEESE

Preparation time:	Serves:	Total cooking time:
15 minutes + marinading	4	12 minutes

90ml (6 tbsp) groundnut oil

5ml (1 tsp) sesame seed oil

1 clove garlic, crushed

30ml (2 tbsp) dry sherry

10ml (2 tsp) dark soy sauce

2 shallots, finely chopped

5ml (1 tsp) sugar

300g (11 oz) Halloumi cheese or tofu, cubed

50g (2 oz) carrots, finely sliced

1 bunch spring onions, chopped

60g (2½ oz) spring greens, finely shredded

110g (4 oz) medium egg noodles, cooked

Freshly ground black pepper

Blend 60ml (4 tbsp) of the groundnut oil with the sesame seed oil, garlic, sherry, soy sauce, shallots and sugar. Stir in the Halloumi cheese or tofu, and marinate for at least 4 hours, preferably overnight. Heat the remaining groundnut oil in a large wok or frying pan, and sauté the carrots for 2 minutes. Add the remaining vegetables and stir fry for 1 minute. Stir in the cheese or tofu together with the marinade and shallots, and fry for 3–4 minutes. Add the cooked noodles and warm through for 1–2 minutes. Season to taste and serve immediately.

MIXED VEGETABLE KORMA

Preparation time:	Serves:	Total cooking time:
15 minutes	4	55 minutes

110g (4 oz) aubergine

2 small carrots, peeled

110g (4 oz) French beans

110g (4 oz) potatoes, peeled

50g (2 oz) freshly grated coconut
or 25g (1 oz) unsweetened desiccated coconut

5ml (1 tsp) salt and 4 fresh green chillies

3 tomatoes, roughly chopped

110g (4 oz) garden peas

30ml (2 tbsp) garam masala

25g (1 oz) creamed coconut

30ml (2 tbsp) fresh coriander leaves, chopped

Chop the aubergine, carrots, beans and potatoes into 4cm x 1cm (1½ x ½ inch) pieces, and put into a flameproof casserole dish. Pour in 225ml (8 fl oz) of boiling water and bring back to the boil. Place the fresh or desiccated coconut, salt and chillies in a food processor with 150ml (5 fl oz) of water, and blend to a fine paste. Stir the paste into the vegetables and add the tomatoes, peas and garam masala. Bring the mixture to the boil. Cover with a lid and transfer to the oven. Bake for 45 minutes, then remove from the oven and stir in the creamed coconut and coriander until the coconut has dissolved. Serve immediately with basmati rice.

Function	Cooking time	Preheating	Shelf position
Fan heat 190°C	45 minutes	No	First

ROASTED MEDITERRANEAN VEGETABLES

VEGETABLE
SIDE DISHES

ROASTED MEDITERRANEAN VEGETABLES

Preparation time:	Serves:	Total cooking time:
15 minutes	4	40 minutes

1 small red pepper, deseeded and quartered

1 small yellow pepper, deseeded and quartered

1 red onion, quartered

1 garlic bulb, sliced horizontally in half

1 fennel bulb, quartered

110ml (4 fl oz) olive oil

50g (2 oz) yellow mild chillies (optional)

1 courgette, sliced diagonally

1 small aubergine, thickly sliced

4 plum tomatoes

110g (4 oz) feta cheese, crumbled

5ml (1 tsp) fresh oregano, chopped

25g (1 oz) pitted black olives

60ml (4 tbsp) extra virgin olive oil

5ml (1 tsp) balsamic vinegar

30ml (2 tbsp) lemon juice

Salt and freshly ground black pepper

Handful of basil leaves, torn

Place the peppers, onion, garlic and fennel in the deep roasting tray. Brush generously with half of the olive oil and roast for 20 minutes. Turn the vegetables and add the chillies, courgette, aubergine and tomatoes. Brush with the rest of the olive oil and roast for a further 20 minutes. Five minutes before the end of the cooking time, sprinkle the feta cheese, oregano and black olives over the vegetables and cook until the cheese begins to melt. Meanwhile blend together the extra virgin olive oil, balsamic vinegar, lemon juice and seasoning. Squeeze the soft flesh from 2 roasted garlic cloves, and whisk into the dressing, according to taste. Transfer the vegetables to a warmed serving plate, drizzle the dressing over them, then sprinkle with torn basil leaves. Serve warm or cold with crusty bread.

Function	Cooking time	Preheating	Shelf position
Fan heat 200°C	40 minutes	No	First

FENNEL AU GRATIN

Preparation time:	Serves:	Total cooking time:
5 minutes	4	30 minutes

3 large fennel bulbs

Salt and freshly ground black pepper

40g (1½ oz) butter

50g (2 oz) freshly grated Parmesan

50g (2 oz) mature Cheddar, grated

Trim the tough stalks from each fennel bulb, slice off the base and discard the outer layer if damaged. Quarter the bulbs from top to base. Simmer the fennel in salted water until just tender. Pack closely into a shallow buttered ovenproof dish and season. Dot with the butter and sprinkle the Parmesan and Cheddar evenly over the top. Bake in the oven for about 12 minutes, or until the cheese is melted and golden. Serve immediately as an accompaniment to roasts, or as a starter.

Function	Cooking time	Preheating	Shelf position
Fan grill 190°C	12 minutes	No	Third

ITALIAN STUFFED TOMATOES

Preparation time:	Serves:	Total cooking time:
5 minutes + draining	4	10 minutes

2 large beef tomatoes

50g (2 oz) wholemeal breadcrumbs

1 clove garlic, crushed

45ml (3 tbsp) fresh parsley, chopped

5ml (1 tsp) lemon juice

5ml (1 tsp) dried chillies

Salt and freshly ground black pepper

15 – 30ml (1 – 2 tbsp) virgin olive oil

25g (1 oz) grated Parmesan or other Italian hard cheese

Remove the stalks from the tomatoes and slice in half horizontally. Scoop out the flesh and set aside. Turn the tomato shells upside down and drain for 15 minutes. Meanwhile, mix the breadcrumbs, garlic, parsley, lemon juice, chillies, and 30ml (2 tbsp) of the tomato flesh in a bowl. Season well then stir in 15ml (1 tbsp) of oil. Place the tomatoes the right way up on a baking tray and fill with the stuffing mixture. Sprinkle with the Parmesan and then drizzle over the remaining oil. Grill until lightly browned and serve immediately.

Function	Cooking time	Preheating	Shelf position
Fan grill 175ºC	10 minutes	No	Fourth

GRATIN DAUPHINOIS

Preparation time:	Serves:	Total cooking time:
10 minutes	4	1 hour

700g (1½ lb) baking potatoes and 570ml (1 pint) milk

Fresh bouquet garni (parsley, celery leaves, thyme and a piece of leek, all tied together)

Salt and freshly ground black pepper

25g (1 oz) butter

150ml (5 fl oz) double cream

110g (4 oz) Gruyère cheese, grated

1 clove garlic, halved

2.5ml (½ tsp) freshly grated nutmeg

Parsley to garnish

Peel and slice the potatoes thinly. Rinse and dry them thoroughly. Put the potato slices, milk, bouquet garni, salt, pepper and half the butter into a large saucepan. Bring to the boil, stirring occasionally to prevent sticking. Once boiling, reduce the heat to a simmer and cook for about 10 minutes until the potatoes are just tender. Meanwhile, mix the cream and cheese together and put to one side. Grease the bottom of a shallow ovenproof dish with the remaining butter and garlic. Use a slotted spoon to transfer half the potatoes to the dish. Sprinkle with a pinch of nutmeg and freshly ground pepper. Layer the remaining potatoes in the dish and sprinkle with the remaining nutmeg and pepper. Spread the cream and cheese mixture over the potatoes. Discard the milk and bouquet garni. Bake until the potatoes are tender inside and crisp and golden on top. Garnish with parsley and serve immediately.

Function	Cooking time	Preheating	Shelf position
Fan grill 190ºC	45 minutes	No	Second

BRAISED RED CABBAGE

ROAST NEW POTATOES WITH GARLIC

Preparation time:	Serves:	Total cooking time:
5 minutes	4	35 minutes

450g (1 lb) new potatoes, scrubbed

60ml (4 tbsp) extra virgin olive oil

8 cloves garlic, peeled and some coarse sea salt

12 fresh basil leaves

Parboil the potatoes in salted water for 10 minutes. Heat the oil in a small roasting tin until hot. Add the well drained potatoes and whole cloves of garlic, and baste in the oil. Sprinkle with sea salt. Roast in the oven until the skins are crisp and the centres are soft. Scatter with fresh basil leaves and the soft flesh from 2 roasted garlic cloves just before serving.

Function	Cooking time	Preheating	Shelf position
Fan heat 200ºC	20 minutes	No	First

BUTTERED MANGE TOUT

Preparation time:	Serves:	Total cooking time:
5 minutes	4	15 minutes

1 bunch spring onions and 25g (1 oz) butter

50g (2 oz) smoked bacon, cubed

225g (8 oz) mange tout

Salt and freshly ground black pepper

Roughly chop the spring onions, reserving the green tops. Melt the butter in a saucepan and sauté the bacon. Add the chopped onions to the pan and cook gently for 2 – 3 minutes. Stir in the mange tout and 30ml (2 tbsp) of water. Season with a little salt and plenty of ground black pepper. Cover the saucepan with a lid, and simmer gently for 10 minutes, or until the liquid has almost evaporated and the mange tout are tender. Meanwhile, finely chop the green tops of the spring onions and mix with the mange tout just before serving.

BRAISED RED CABBAGE

Preparation time:	Serves:	Total cooking time:
10 minutes	4 – 6	1 hr – 1 hr 30 mins

25g (1 oz) butter

Half an onion, sliced

1 small sharp apple, peeled and sliced

Half a red cabbage, shredded

25g (1 oz) soft brown sugar

50g (2 oz) sultanas

150ml (5 fl oz) vegetable stock

Salt and freshly ground black pepper

Melt the butter in a large flameproof casserole and fry the onion until soft and translucent. Add the apple and sauté for 1 minute. Stir in the red cabbage and cook for a further minute. Add the remaining ingredients, mixing well. Cover with a tight-fitting lid, and braise slowly in the oven until the cabbage is tender. Check the cabbage occasionally to ensure it is not drying out, and top up with a little boiling water if necessary.

Function	Cooking time	Preheating	Shelf position
Fan heat 175ºC	1 hr – 1 hr 30 mins	No	First

VICHY CARROTS

Preparation time:	Serves:	Total cooking time:
5 minutes	4	35 – 40 minutes

500g (1¼ lb) baby carrots

Salt and freshly ground black pepper

75ml (3 fl oz) chicken or vegetable stock

25g (1 oz) butter

Chopped fresh parsley to garnish

Put the carrots in a large saucepan of boiling salted water. Bring back to the boil and cook for 1 minute. Drain and plunge into cold water to prevent further cooking. Place in a deep 1 litre (1¾ pint) ovenproof dish. Pour in the stock and dot with butter. Season and cover tightly. Bake in the oven until the carrots are cooked but still retain some bite (al dente). Stir once during the cooking time. Serve garnished with parsley.

Function	Cooking time	Preheating	Shelf position
Fan heat 160°C	25 – 30 minutes	No	First

ROASTED ROOT VEGETABLES

Preparation time:	Serves:	Total cooking time:
10 minutes	4	45 minutes

75ml (3 fl oz) olive oil or roast meat fat and juices

2 medium potatoes, peeled and halved
or 8 even-sized new potatoes, scrubbed

1 sweet potato, peeled and quartered

2 medium sized parsnips, peeled and halved

Half a small swede, peeled and cut into wedges

1 large red onion, peeled and quartered

8 cloves of garlic, with skins on

Coarse sea salt and freshly ground black pepper

30 – 45ml (2 – 3 tbsp) clear honey (optional)

Chopped fresh herbs to garnish

Pour the oil or meat fat into a medium-sized roasting tin or the deep roasting tray. Heat in the oven until very hot. Add the potatoes and parsnips, baste well, and roast for 10 minutes. Add the remaining vegetables, baste and sprinkle generously with coarse sea salt and black pepper, then toss in honey if liked. Roast in the oven for 35 minutes until the vegetables are rich golden brown and still soft inside. Drain well on kitchen paper, then serve garnished with chopped fresh herbs.

Function	Cooking time	Preheating	Shelf position
Auto roast 200°C	35 minutes	No	First

ROAST POTATOES

Preparation time:	Serves:	Total cooking time:
10 minutes	4	40 minutes

900g (2 lb) potatoes, peeled, cut and parboiled

90ml (6 tbsp) oil or meat fat

Pour the oil or fat into a roasting tin and heat in the oven until very hot. Add the potatoes and baste well. Roast for about 40 minutes, until golden in colour, crisp on the outside and soft inside. NB: if the potatoes are to be roasted with the meat, place the tin underneath the joint on the wire rack to self-baste in the meat juices. Alternatively, place around the meat, basting occasionally.

Function	Cooking time	Preheating	Shelf position
Fan heat 220°C	40 minutes	Yes	First

PUDDINGS
HOT & COLD

APRICOT PUDDINGS
WITH TOFFEE NUT SAUCE

Preparation time:	Serves:	Total cooking time:
10 minutes	8	25 – 30 minutes

10g (¹/₂ oz) caster sugar

175g (6 oz) ready to eat dried apricots, chopped

175ml (6 fl oz) boiling water

2.5ml (¹/₂ tsp) vanilla essence

10ml (2 tsp) coffee essence

2.5ml (¹/₂ tsp) bicarbonate of soda

10ml (2 tsp) dark rum

200g (7 oz) butter and 150g (5 oz) caster sugar

2 eggs, beaten

175g (6 oz) self-raising flour, sifted

175g (6 oz) soft light brown sugar

75ml (5 tbsp) double cream

25g (1oz) walnuts, chopped

Liberally grease 8 x 175g (6 oz) dariole moulds and coat thoroughly with caster sugar. Place the apricots in a bowl and cover with the boiling water. Stir in the vanilla and coffee essences, bicarbonate of soda and rum, then place to one side. Cream 75g (3 oz) of the butter and the sugar together until pale and fluffy, then gradually add the eggs, beating well after each addition. Using a metal spoon, lightly fold in the sifted flour, followed by the apricot mixture (including the liquid). Divide equally between the moulds and place on a baking tray. Bake until the puddings are well risen, golden brown and firm to the touch. Leave to cool for 5 minutes before turning out.

To make the sauce, place the brown sugar, cream and the remaining butter in a saucepan. Stir over a gentle heat until the sauce is smooth and has thickened to a creamy consistency. Remove from the heat and continue stirring until the sugar has dissolved. Add the chopped walnuts. Pour the toffee sauce over the apricot puddings before serving.

Function	Cooking time	Preheating	Shelf position
Fan heat 190°C	20 – 25 minutes	No	First

CREAMY RICE PUDDING

Preparation time:	Serves:	Total cooking time:
5 minutes	4	50 minutes

40g (1¹/₂ oz) pudding rice

25g (1 oz) caster sugar

275ml (¹/₂ pint) milk

275ml (¹/₂ pint) single cream

10g (¹/₂ oz) butter

1 cinnamon stick or 5ml (1 tsp) ground nutmeg

Generously butter an 850ml (1½ pint) high-sided ovenproof dish. Place the rice and sugar in the dish. Pour in the milk and cream, and add the butter and cinnamon stick, or sprinkle the surface with nutmeg. Bake on the wire rack for 25 minutes at 200°C, or until the pudding is bubbling and a skin is beginning to form. Reduce the heat to 170°C and cook for 25 minutes until the rice is soft and creamy and the pudding is golden. Remove the cinammon stick, if used, and serve hot.

Function	Cooking time	Preheating	Shelf position
Fan heat 200°+170°C	25mins + 25mins	Yes	Second

TIPSY FRUIT COMPOTE

Preparation time:	Serves:	Total cooking time:
10 minutes	4 – 6	25 minutes

250g (9 oz) prunes, stoned

275g (10 oz) dried apricots

50g (2 oz) sultanas

75g (3 oz) dried apple

1 cinnamon stick

60ml (4 tbsp) whisky

570ml (1 pint) unsweetened orange juice

15ml (1 level tbsp) soft brown sugar

Rind of 1 lemon, cut into fine shreds

3 bananas, peeled and sliced

Place all the fruit except the bananas into an ovenproof dish with the cinnamon stick. Combine the whisky, orange juice, sugar and lemon rind. Pour over the fruit. Cover with foil and bake in the oven until the fruit is tender. Leave to cool. Stir in the sliced bananas before serving warm or cold. Alternatively, arrange the bananas over the fruit, sprinkle with a little demerara sugar and place under a preheated grill to brown and crisp the surface. Delicious served with creamy rice pudding (see page 97).

Function	Cooking time	Preheating	Shelf position
Fan heat 160ºC	25 minutes	No	First

BAKED ALASKA

Preparation time:	Serves:	Total cooking time:
5 minutes + marinading	6	3 – 5 minutes

225g (8 oz) fresh or frozen raspberries

30ml (2 tbsp) Drambuie

One 20cm (8 inch) baked sponge flan case

4 egg whites, at room temperature

175g (6 oz) caster sugar

425ml (3/4 pint) block hard-frozen vanilla ice cream

Place the fresh or defrosted raspberries in a shallow dish and sprinkle over the liqueur. Cover and leave to marinate for 30 minutes, turning occasionally. Place the sponge on a large ovenproof serving dish and spoon the raspberries with all their juices into the flan case. Place the egg whites in a clean bowl and whisk until the mixture stands in stiff peaks. Add half of the sugar and whisk until the mixture is thick and glossy. Add the remaining sugar and fold in using a metal spoon. Fit a large piping bag with a large star vegetable nozzle and fill with the meringue mixture. Place the block of ice cream on top of the raspberries. Completely cover the ice cream and sponge with piped meringue, ensuring that there are no gaps. Place the Alaska in the oven, and bake on the wire rack until the meringue is lightly browned. (Watch the meringue carefully, as it burns easily). Do not overcook or the ice cream will become too soft. Serve immediately.

Function	Cooking time	Preheating	Shelf position
Conventional 210ºC	3 – 5 minutes	Yes	Second

CHOCOLATE COINTREAU SOUFFLE

Preparation time:	Serves:	Total cooking time:
15 minutes	4	30 – 35 minutes

5ml (1 tsp) melted butter

60ml (4 tbsp) caster sugar

150ml (5 fl oz) warm patisserie cream,
omitting the liqueur (see page 135)

2 egg yolk

175g (6 oz) plain chocolate

20ml (4 tsp) Cointreau and the grated rind of 1 orange

6 egg whites and 5ml (1 tsp) lemon juice

Icing sugar to dust

With a pastry brush, evenly coat the inside of a 1.2 litre (2 pint) soufflé dish with the melted butter. Sprinkle 30ml (2 tbsp) of the sugar into the bottom of the dish and rotate it until the whole dish is coated with sugar, tipping out any excess. In a bowl whisk together the warmed patisserie cream and egg yolks. Melt the chocolate over a pan of simmering water, add the Cointreau and orange rind. Pour over the egg yolk mixture, whisking well. Beat the egg whites until they form soft peaks, add the rest of the sugar and lemon juice and whisk again until firm but not stiff. Whisk a quarter of the egg white into the chocolate mixture, then lightly fold in the rest, using a metal spoon. Pour into the soufflé dish up to the top, leaving a clean inside rim. Bake on the wire rack until well risen with a crisp top shell and a foamy centre. Dust with icing sugar before serving.

Function	Cooking time	Preheating	Shelf position
Conventional 190°C	25 – 30 minutes	Yes	Second

TROPICAL FRUIT CLAFOUTIS

Preparation time:	Serves:	Total cooking time:
10 minutes + standing	4	30 – 40 minutes

1 vanilla pod

3 eggs, room temperature

175g (6 oz) caster sugar or vanilla sugar

175g (6 oz) plain flour, sifted

Pinch of salt

175ml (6 fl oz) crème fraîche

175ml (6 fl oz) whole milk

15ml (1 tbsp) brandy

2 bananas, sliced

15ml (1 tbsp) lemon juice

4 pineapple rings, chopped

Lightly butter and sugar a 17.5 x 22.5cm (7 x 9 inch) baking dish. Cut the vanilla pod in half lengthways and scrape the seeds into a bowl. Add the eggs and whisk well. Stir in the sugar, flour, salt, crème fraîche, milk and brandy. Mix until well blended, then leave the batter to stand for 10 minutes. Dip the banana slices in lemon juice, and arrange with the pineapple in the base of the prepared dish. Pour the batter over the fruit and bake in the oven until the mixture is rich golden brown and lightly set.
NB: the remaining vanilla pod can be used to prepare vanilla sugar. Any soft fruit in season can be used for the clafoutis, e.g. cherries, plums, dessert pears.

Function	Cooking time	Preheating	Shelf position
Fan heat 200°C	30 – 40 minutes	No	First

BAKED APPLES

Preparation time: 10 minutes	Serves: 4	Total cooking time: 25 – 35 minutes

25g (1 oz) soft brown sugar

25g (1 oz) dates, chopped

10g (½ oz) walnuts, chopped

25g (1 oz) glacé cherries, chopped

30ml (2 tbsp) brandy

30ml (2 tbsp) mincemeat

15ml (1 tbsp) clear honey

15ml (1 tbsp) lemon juice

4 medium cooking apples

30ml (2 tbsp) water

10ml (2 tsp) cinnamon

Place the sugar, dates, walnuts, cherries, brandy, mincemeat, honey and lemon juice in a bowl and mix well. Wash and core the apples and make a shallow cut through the skin around the centre. Stand the apples on a lightly greased baking tray and fill them with the mixture. Pour the water around the apples and sprinkle with the cinnamon. Bake until the apples are soft when tested with a skewer. Serve hot with custard or patisserie cream (see page 135).

Function	Cooking time	Preheating	Shelf position
Fan heat 160ºC	25 – 35 minutes	No	First

EVE'S PUDDING

Preparation time: 10 minutes	Serves: 4 – 6	Total cooking time: 45 minutes

450g (1 lb) eating apples, peeled and cored

25g (1 oz) demerara sugar

Grated rind of 1 lemon

150g (5 oz) butter

150g (5 oz) caster sugar

2 eggs, beaten

150g (5 oz) self-raising flour, sifted

15 – 30ml (1 – 2 tbsp) milk

Slice the apples thinly and place in a greased 1.5 litre (2½ pint) ovenproof dish. Sprinkle with the demerara sugar and lemon rind, then add 15ml (1 tbsp) of water. Cream the butter and caster sugar together until light and fluffy. Gradually add the eggs, beating well after each addition, then fold in the flour. Stir in enough milk to give a dropping consistency, and spoon the mixture over the apples. Bake on the wire rack until the apples are tender and a skewer inserted into the centre of the pudding comes out clean. Serve hot with custard.

Function	Cooking time	Preheating	Shelf position
Conventional 180ºC	45 minutes	Yes	Second

BAKED APPLES

GOLDEN SYRUP PUDDING

MARSALA BREAD & BUTTER PUDDING

Preparation time:	Serves:	Total cooking time:
10 minutes + resting	4	40 minutes

350ml (12 fl oz) milk

150ml (5 fl oz) single cream

15 – 30ml (1 – 2 tbsp) Marsala

4 eggs

2.5ml (½ tsp) vanilla essence

7 thick slices of bread

Butter for spreading

110g (4 oz) demerara sugar

150g (5 oz) sultanas

5ml (1 tsp) ground nutmeg

Apricot jam to glaze

Pour the milk, cream and Marsala into a saucepan. Heat gently to simmering point, but do not allow to boil. Whisk the eggs and vanilla essence together, then gradually whisk into the milk and cream. Remove the crusts from the bread, and butter on one side. Cut the bread into strips, arrange a single layer in the bottom of a greased deep pie dish, and sprinkle with some of the sugar and sultanas. Continue layering until all the bread has been used, then pour the egg mixture into the dish and sprinkle with nutmeg. Leave to rest for 10 minutes to allow the liquid to soak in. Bake in the oven on the wire rack until browned and lightly set. Leave to rest for a few minutes, then glaze with warmed apricot jam and serve.

Function	Cooking time	Preheating	Shelf position
Conventional 180°C	35 – 40 minutes	Yes	Second

GOLDEN SYRUP PUDDING

Preparation time:	Serves:	Total cooking time:
10 minutes	4 – 6	1 hour 35 minutes

175g (6 oz) self-raising flour

Pinch of salt

50g (2 oz) butter

25g (1 oz) caster sugar

90ml (6 tbsp) milk

90ml (6 tbsp) golden syrup

45ml (3 tbsp) water

30ml (2 tbsp) lemon juice

Grease a 1.2 litre (2 pint) pudding basin. Sieve the flour and salt into a large mixing bowl. Rub in the butter until the mixture resembles fine breadcrumbs, then stir in the sugar. Make a well in the centre, add the milk and mix thoroughly. Put 30ml (2 tbsp) of the syrup in the bottom of the basin and spoon the mixture on top. Cover with greaseproof paper and secure with string, before steaming for 1 hour 30 minutes. Turn out onto a warmed plate to serve. To make the sauce, warm the remaining syrup and water gently in a saucepan, stirring well, and simmer for 2-3 minutes. Add the lemon juice and pour the sauce over the pudding just before serving.

PROFITEROLES

Preparation time:	Serves:	Total cooking time:
10 minutes	4 – 6	20 – 25 minutes

150ml (¼ pint) water

50g (2 oz) butter

75g (3 oz) plain flour, sifted

2 eggs, lightly beaten

150ml (¼ pint) whipped cream
or 200ml (7 fl oz) patisserie cream (see page 135)

Rich chocolate or coffee cream sauce (see page 135)

Icing sugar to dust

Place the water and butter in a saucepan. Heat until the butter melts, then bring to the boil. Remove the pan from the heat and quickly tip the flour in all at once. Beat until the paste is smooth and forms a ball. Be careful not to over-beat at this stage. Allow to cool a little. Add the eggs, a little at a time, beating vigorously to trap as much air as possible. Continue beating until the mixture is glossy. Pile the paste into a piping bag fitted with a 1cm (½ inch) plain nozzle. Pipe small balls of the mixture onto a lightly greased baking tray. Bake until golden brown and crisp. Make a small slit in the side of each bun to allow the steam to escape, then leave to cool on a wire rack. To serve, fill a piping bag with whipped cream or patisserie cream and pipe into each profiterole. Pile them into a serving dish, and cover with rich chocolate or coffee cream sauce. Dust with icing sugar before serving.

Function	Cooking time	Preheating	Shelf position
Fan heat 190ºC	20 – 25 minutes	No	Second

LEMON MERINGUE PIE

Preparation time:	Serves:	Total cooking time:
10 minutes + chilling	4 – 6	40 minutes

175g (6 oz) plain flour with a pinch of salt

75g (3 oz) butter

45ml (3 level tbsp) cornflour

Grated rind and juice of 2 lemons

200g (7 oz) caster sugar

2 eggs, separated

For the pastry, sift the plain flour and salt into a bowl. Rub in the butter until the mixture resembles fine breadcrumbs. Mix in 30–45ml (2–3 tbsp) iced water to give a firm dough. Roll out the pastry on a lightly floured surface, and use to line a lightly greased 17.5cm (7 inch) flan dish. Cover the base with foil and fill with baking beans. Bake blind on the intensive bake function until the pastry base is dry. Remove the baking beans for the final 10 minutes. Measure 150ml (5 fl oz) water into a small saucepan. Mix the cornflour to a paste using a little water. Pour into the pan along with the lemon rind and juice. Bring slowly to the boil, stirring until the mixture thickens. Stir in 110g (4 oz) of sugar. Remove from the heat, allow to cool slightly. Beat in the egg yolks and pour into the pastry case. In a separate bowl, whisk the egg whites until stiff. Add half the remaining sugar and whisk until the mixture is thick and glossy, then fold in the rest. Pile the meringue on top of the lemon filling. Bake on fan heat for 10 to 15 minutes until the meringue is crisp and lightly browned.

Function	Cooking time	Preheating	Shelf position
Int. bake 200ºC	15 – 20 minutes	Yes	First

Function	Cooking time	Preheating	Shelf position
Fan heat 180ºC	10 – 15 minutes	Yes	First

PROFITEROLES

TRADITIONAL APPLE PIE

QUEEN OF PUDDINGS

Preparation time:	Serves:	Total cooking time:
10 minutes	4 – 6	30 minutes

75g (3 oz) caster sugar

200g (7 oz) breadcrumbs

Grated rind of 1 lemon

25g (1 oz) butter

275ml (½ pint) milk

2 eggs, separated

45ml (3 tbsp) raspberry jam
or 50g (2 oz) chopped fresh raspberries

Grease an 850ml (1½ pint) oval pie dish. Mix together 50g (2 oz) of the sugar, the breadcrumbs and lemon rind in a bowl. Melt the butter and milk together in a saucepan, and pour over the breadcrumb mixture. Stir in the beaten egg yolks and pour into the pie dish. Bake for about 15 minutes until just set, then leave to cool slightly. Spread the top of the pudding with warmed jam or scatter with fresh raspberries. Whisk the egg whites until stiff. Whisk in half the remaining sugar, then gently fold in the rest. Pile the meringue on top of the pudding and bake for a further 10 minutes until lightly browned. Equally delicious served hot or cold.

Function	Cooking time	Preheating	Shelf position
Conventional 180°C	25 minutes	Yes	Second

TRADITIONAL APPLE PIE

Preparation time:	Serves:	Total cooking time:
15 minutes + chilling	6	45 minutes

225g (8 oz) plain flour and a pinch of salt

125g (4½ oz) butter

10ml (2 tsp) caster sugar

45ml (3 tbsp) water

900g (2 lb) cooking apples, peeled, cored and sliced

125g (4½oz) light brown sugar

2.5ml (½ level tsp) each ground cinnamon & ground nutmeg

Finely grated rind and juice of half a lemon

Milk and caster sugar to glaze

For the pastry, sift the flour and salt into a mixing bowl. Rub in the butter until the mixture resembles fine breadcrumbs, then add the caster sugar. Stir in enough water to make a firm dough. Wrap the pastry in clingfilm and chill in the refrigerator for 30 minutes. On a lightly floured surface, roll out a little more than half the pastry and use to line a greased 22.5cm (9 inch) pie plate. Moisten the rim of the pastry with a little water. Put the apple slices in a bowl and stir in the brown sugar, spices, lemon rind and juice. Spoon into the pie dish. Roll out the remaining pastry and use to cover the pie. Decorate with pastry leaves, and make a small slit in the centre of the pastry lid for the steam to escape. Brush with milk and sprinkle over a little caster sugar. Bake on the wire rack for 15 minutes at 200°C, then reduce to 180°C and cook for a further 30 minutes until the pastry is crisp and golden. Serve hot or cold with cream or custard.

Function	Cooking time	Preheating	Shelf position
Conv. 200+180°C	15 + 30 minutes	Yes	Second

PEAR & ALMOND FLAN

Preparation time:	Serves:	Total cooking time:
15 minutes + chilling	4 – 6	25 – 30 minutes

Pastry	110g (4 oz) plain flour with a pinch of salt
	50g (2 oz) butter and 25g (1 oz) caster sugar
	1 egg, lightly beaten
Filling	110g (4 oz) butter
	110g (4 oz) caster sugar
	2 eggs, lightly beaten
	50g (2 oz) self-raising flour
	50g (2 oz) ground almonds
	5 – 10ml (1 – 2 tsp) almond essence
	2 firm pears, peeled and sliced
	Flaked almonds to decorate

For the pastry, mix together the flour and salt in a bowl. Rub in the butter until the mixture resembles fine breadcrumbs, and stir in the sugar. Mix in the egg to give a fairly firm dough. Wrap in clingfilm and leave to chill in the refrigerator for 30 minutes. Roll out on a floured surface, and use to line a lightly greased 20cm (8 inch) flan dish. Rest the pastry in the refrigerator for a further 15 minutes. For the filling, cream the butter and sugar together until pale and fluffy. Gradually add the eggs, beating well after each addition. If the mixture begins to curdle, sift in a little flour. Fold in the remaining flour, together with the almonds and almond essence. Spread the mixture into the pastry case. Arrange the pear slices on top and decorate with flaked almonds. Bake until the flan is golden brown and firm to the touch.

Function	Cooking time	Preheating	Shelf position
Int. bake 180°C	25 – 30 minutes	No	First

RHUBARB & GINGER CRUMBLE

Preparation time:	Serves:	Total cooking time:
10 minutes	4 – 6	30 – 35 minutes

700g (1½ lb) rhubarb, trimmed
125g (4½ oz) demerara sugar
5ml (1 tsp) ground ginger
Finely grated rind and juice of 1 orange
225g (8 oz) plain flour
125g (4½ oz) butter
50g (2 oz) soft brown sugar

Cut the rhubarb into 2.5cm (1 inch) pieces, and place in a 22.5cm (9 inch) flan dish. Mix together the demerara sugar, ginger and orange rind, and sprinkle over the fruit. Pour the orange juice over the rhubarb.

For the crumble, sift the flour into a bowl and rub in the butter until the mixture resembles fine breadcrumbs. Stir in the soft brown sugar, then spoon the crumble over the rhubarb. Bake until the crumble is golden brown. Serve hot or cold with custard or cream.

Function	Cooking time	Preheating	Shelf position
Fan heat 170°C	30 – 35 minutes	No	First

SPICED RED PLUMS

Preparation time:	Serves:	Total cooking time:
10 minutes + marinading	4	15 minutes

75g (3 oz) soft brown sugar

150ml (5 fl oz) port

2.5ml (½ tsp) ground mixed spice

Pinch of ground nutmeg

3 cloves

5cm (2 inch) cinnamon stick

150ml (¼ pint) water

450g (1 lb) ripe red plums, halved and stoned

Place the sugar, port, spices and water into a large shallow saucepan and heat gently until the sugar dissolves. Bring to the boil and simmer for 1 minute. Add the plums to the syrup and bring slowly back to the boil. Cover the pan and simmer gently until the plums are just tender. This may take as little as 2–3 minutes, depending on the ripeness of the fruit. Do not overcook, as the fruit will continue to soften in the heat of the syrup. Pour into a serving dish and cool. Cover with clingfilm and leave tomarinade in a refrigerator for at least 24 hours. Serve chilled, or reheat gently and serve warm with frozen meringue cream (see page 135).

CREME BRULEE

Preparation time:	Serves:	Total cooking time:
5 minutes + chilling	6	40 minutes

275ml (½ pint) double cream

275ml (½ pint) single cream

4 egg yolks

75g (3 oz) caster sugar

5ml (1 tsp) vanilla essence

Put the cream into a saucepan and warm gently over a low heat to simmering point, but do not allow to boil. Place the egg yolks, 25g (1 oz) of the caster sugar and the vanilla essence in a mixing bowl and whisk thoroughly. Stir in the warmed cream and whisk thoroughly. Pour into 6 individual ramekin dishes and place them in the deep roasting tray or suitable dish. Pour in sufficient hot water to come halfway up the sides of the dishes. Bake in the oven for about 35 minutes, or until just set. Chill in the refrigerator for several hours, preferably overnight. Heat the grill to 280°C. Completely cover the top of each custard with the rest of the sugar. Place the dishes as close to the grill as possible and heat until the sugar begins to caramelize. Serve with fresh fruit.

Function	Cooking time	Preheating	Shelf position
Fan heat 130°C	35 – 40 minutes	No	First

Function	Cooking time	Preheating	Shelf position
Grill 280°C	Few seconds	Yes	Fourth

TREACLE TART

PECAN PIE

Preparation time:	Serves:	Total cooking time:
15 minutes + chilling	4 – 6	30 minutes

Pastry	110g (4 oz) plain flour
	50g (2 oz) butter
	25g (1 oz) caster sugar
	1 egg, beaten
Filling	75g (3 oz) light brown sugar
	75ml (3 fl oz) golden syrup
	75ml (3 fl oz) maple syrup
	3 eggs
	15ml (1 tbsp) milk
	50g (2 oz) butter
	2.5ml (½ tsp) vanilla essence
	100g (3½ oz) pecan nuts
	50g (2 oz) cake crumbs

To make the pastry, place the flour in a bowl and rub in the butter until the mixture resembles fine breadcrumbs. Stir in the sugar, then add the egg and mix well to give a firm dough. Wrap in clingfilm and chill in the refrigerator for 30 minutes. Roll out the pastry on a well floured surface, and use to line a lightly greased 20cm (8 inch) flan dish. For the filling, place the sugar and syrups in a saucepan and bring to the boil. Cook for 2–3 minutes, then leave to cool slightly. Beat the eggs and milk together in a bowl. Pour the hot syrup slowly over the egg mixture, stirring continuously. Add the butter and vanilla essence, and stir until the butter has melted and the sugar has dissolved. Chop half of the pecan nuts and sprinkle them over the pastry case. Stir the cake crumbs into the syrup mixture, then pour this into the pastry. Decorate with the remaining whole nuts, and bake in the oven until the pastry is golden brown and the filling is set. Serve with patisserie cream (see page 135).

Function	Cooking time	Preheating	Shelf position
Int. bake 190°C	25 – 30 minutes	No	First

TREACLE TART

Preparation time:	Serves:	Total cooking time:
10 minutes + chilling	4	20 – 25 minutes

110g (4 oz) plain flour
50g (2 oz) butter
25g (1 oz) caster sugar
1 egg, lightly beaten
90ml (6 tbsp) golden syrup
50g (2 oz) fresh white breadcrumbs
Grated rind of half a lemon

Sift the flour into a bowl and rub in the butter until the mixture resembles fine breadcrumbs. Stir in the sugar. Add the egg and mix to give a firm dough. Cover with clingfilm and chill for 30 minutes. Roll out the pastry on a well floured surface and use to line a lightly greased 17.5cm (7 inch) flan dish. Chill for a further 10 minutes. Mix the golden syrup, breadcrumbs and lemon rind together, and spoon the mixture into the pastry case. Any remaining pastry may be cut into strips and arranged over the filling in a lattice pattern. Bake in the oven until the pastry is golden brown. Serve warm or cold.

Function	Cooking time	Preheating	Shelf position
Int. bake 180°C	20 – 25 minutes	No	First

WHITE CHOCOLATE ROULADE

Preparation time:	Serves:	Total cooking time:
5 minutes + cooling	6 – 8	30 minutes

6 large eggs, separated

225g (8 oz) vanilla sugar*

50g (2 oz) cocoa powder

150g (5 oz) white chocolate

425ml (3/4 pint) double cream

30ml (2 tbsp) dark rum

Icing sugar to dredge

Line a 33 x 20cm (13 x 8 inch) Swiss roll tin with silicone paper, cutting diagonally into the corners to give a neat lining. Put the egg yolks and vanilla sugar (*or caster sugar and a few drops of vanilla essence) into a bowl, and whisk until pale and thick enough to retain a trail on the surface when the beaters are lifted. Sift the cocoa powder into the egg mixture and fold in lightly using a metal spoon. In a separate bowl, whisk the egg whites until stiff but not dry, and fold carefully into the chocolate mixture. Pour gently into the prepared tin and spread evenly. Bake until the surface springs back when lightly pressed. Remove from the oven and allow to cool slightly. Meanwhile, place a sheet of greaseproof paper over a damp tea towel and dredge the paper with icing sugar. Turn the roulade onto the paper and carefully remove the silicone paper. Trim the edges with a knife and roll up the roulade with the sugared paper inside. Leave to cool for 20 minutes. To make the filling, break the chocolate into pieces and melt slowly in a bowl over a pan of simmering water. Stir in 45ml (3 tbsp) cream and the rum. Allow to cool slightly. Unroll the roulade, remove the paper and spread with the chocolate sauce.

Lightly whip the remaining cream and spread over the roulade. Roll up again and dredge with icing sugar before serving.

Function	Cooking time	Preheating	Shelf position
Fan heat 200°C	25 minutes	No	First

STRAWBERRY PAVLOVA

Preparation time:	Serves:	Total cooking time:
10 minutes	4 – 6	60 – 75 minutes

3 egg whites

175g (6 oz) caster sugar

5ml (1 level tsp) cornflour

5ml (1 tsp) vinegar

2.5ml (1/2 tsp) vanilla essence

275ml (1/2 pint) double cream

225g (8 oz) strawberries, hulled

Draw a 22.5cm (9 inch) circle on non-stick paper and place on a baking tray. Whisk the egg whites until stiff but not dry. Gradually whisk in half the sugar, then gently fold in the remainder, together with the cornflour, vinegar and vanilla essence. Spread the mixture over the circle, forming a lip around the edges. Bake until the meringue is crisp on the outside and slightly soft inside. Leave until cold. Carefully remove the paper and place the meringue on a serving plate. Whip the cream until thick and pile into the meringue. Decorate with the strawberries.

Function	Cooking time	Preheating	Shelf position
Fan heat 100°C	60 – 75 minutes	No	First

STRAWBERRY PAVLOVA

BLUEBERRY MUFFINS

CAKES, BISCUITS
& BREAD

FARMHOUSE FRUIT CAKE

Preparation time:	Makes:	Total cooking time:
10 minutes	12 slices	1 hr 15 – 1 hr 30 mins

225g (8 oz) wholemeal flour

225g (8 oz) plain flour

5ml (1 tsp) ground mixed spice and 5ml (1 tsp) cinnamon

5ml (1 tsp) bicarbonate of soda

175g (6 oz) unsalted butter

225g (8 oz) caster sugar

110g (4 oz) sultanas and 110g (4 oz) raisins

75g (3 oz) glacé cherries, chopped

45ml (3 tbsp) mixed peel, chopped

1 egg, lightly beaten

275ml ($\frac{1}{2}$ pint) milk

Grease and base line a 20cm (8 inch) square cake tin. Sift together the flours, spices and bicarbonate of soda into a bowl. Rub in the butter until the mixture resembles fine breadcrumbs. Stir in the sugar, fruit and peel. Make a well in the centre and pour in the egg and a little of the milk. Gradually work in the dry ingredients, adding more milk if necessary to obtain a dropping consistency. Spoon the mixture into the prepared tin, making a hollow in the centre with the back of a spoon. Bake on the wire rack until golden brown and firm to the touch. Cover with grease-proof paper after 45 minutes to prevent over-browning. Allow to cool slightly before turning onto a wire rack. The cake should be slightly moist. For a drier cake, extend the cooking time by 5 minutes.

Function	Cooking time	Preheating	Shelf position
Conventional 160°C	1 hr 15 – 30 mins	Yes	Second

VICTORIA SANDWICH CAKE

Preparation time:	Makes:	Total cooking time:
10 minutes	6 slices	20 – 25 minutes

175g (6 oz) unsalted butter

175g (6 oz) caster sugar

3 eggs, beaten

Vanilla essence

175g (6 oz) self-raising flour, sifted

Jam

Icing sugar, sifted

Lightly grease and base line 2 x 17.5cm (7 inch) sandwich tins. Cream the butter and sugar together until light and fluffy. Add the eggs gradually, beating well after each addition, then stir in a few drops of vanilla essence. Gently fold in the flour using a metal spoon. Divide the mixture between the prepared tins, and level the surface. Bake until golden, well risen and springy to the touch. Turn out and cool on a wire rack. When the sponges are cold, sandwich together with jam and sift a little icing sugar over the top.

Function	Cooking time	Preheating	Shelf position
Fan heat 160°C	20 – 25 minutes	No	First

APPLE & CINNAMON CAKE

Preparation time:	Makes:	Total cooking time:
15 minutes	8 slices	30 – 35 minutes

110g (4 oz) butter

110g (4 oz) caster sugar

2 eggs, beaten

5ml (1 tsp) lemon juice

110g (4 oz) plain flour

10ml (2 tsp) baking powder

Pinch of salt

15ml (1 tbsp) milk

1 crisp apple, cored and thinly sliced

10g (½ oz) butter, melted

15ml (1 tbsp) brown sugar

5ml (1 tsp) cinnamon

Grease a 20cm (8 inch) round cake tin. Cream the butter and sugar together in a bowl until light and fluffy. Whisk in the eggs a little at a time, then beat in the lemon juice. Sift the flour, baking powder and salt together, and fold into the mixture with the milk. Spoon the mixture into the prepared tin. Arrange the sliced apples over the surface. Drizzle a little melted butter over the apples and sprinkle with brown sugar and cinnamon to taste. Bake until golden brown, well risen and springy to the touch.

Function	Cooking time	Preheating	Shelf position
Fan heat 160°C	30 – 35 minutes	No	First

RICH FRUIT CAKE

Preparation time:	Makes:	Total cooking time:
15 minutes	16 slices	2hrs 30 mins– 3 hrs

110g (4 oz) glacé cherries

50g (2 oz) whole almonds, blanched

275g (10 oz) plain flour

110g (4 oz) each of raisins and currants

110g (4 oz) sultanas and 75g (3 oz) chopped mixed peel

225g (8 oz) butter

225g (8 oz) soft dark brown sugar and 4 eggs, lightly beaten

5ml (1 tsp) mixed spice and 60ml (4 tbsp) brandy

Grease and line a 20cm (8 inch) cake tin, using a double thickness of greaseproof paper. Tie a double band of brown paper around the outside. Wash and halve the glacé cherries and chop the nuts, reserving a few whole nuts for decoration. Sieve the flour into a bowl and mix the fruit in with the flour. Cream together the butter and sugar in a large bowl until pale and fluffy. Gradually beat in the eggs. Fold in the flour, fruit, peel, spice and nuts. Add 30ml (2 tbsp) of the brandy and spoon the mixture into the lined tin, making a slight hollow in the centre. Arrange the remaining almonds on top. Bake on the wire rack until the top is golden brown, then cover the cake with brown paper to avoid over-browning. After 1 hour 40 minutes, reduce the temperature to 130°C and continue to cook for the remaining time, or until a skewer inserted into the centre comes out clean. When cooked, turn out on to a wire rack and leave to cool. Pierce the surface with a fine skewer, drizzle the remaining brandy over the cake and store for 1 month to allow the flavours to mature.

Function	Cooking time	Preheating	Shelf position
Conv. 150°+130°C	1 hr 40 + 45 mins	Yes	Second

RICH FRUIT CAKE

BLACK FOREST GATEAU

Preparation time:	Serves:	Total cooking time:
10 minutes	8 – 10	25 – 30 minutes

Flour and caster sugar to dust

4 eggs, lightly beaten and 110g (4 oz) caster sugar

75g (3 oz) plain flour and 25g (1 oz) cocoa powder, sifted

450g (1 lb) bottled black cherries in light syrup, pitted

60ml (4 tbsp) Kirsch

425ml (3/4 pint) double cream

110g (4 oz) luxury plain chocolate, coarsely grated

Grease and base line a 22.5cm (9 inch) round cake tin, and dust with flour and caster sugar. Put the eggs and sugar into a bowl resting on a saucepan of hot water. Whisk until the mixture is stiff enough to leave a trail when the whisk is lifted. Remove from the heat and continue whisking until cold. Sift the flour and cocoa onto the mixture and lightly fold in using a metal spoon. Pour the mixture into the prepared tin. Bake until well risen and springy to the touch. Turn out and cool on a wire rack. Drain the cherries and mix 75ml (5 tbsp) of the juice with the Kirsch. Split the cake into three layers. Place a layer on a flat plate and spoon over 45ml (3 tbsp) of the cherry syrup. Whip the cream until it holds its shape, and spread one third over the sponge layer. Reserve a few cherries for decoration and scatter half the remainder over the cream. Repeat the layers of sponge, syrup, cream and cherries, finishing with the third cake round. Spoon over the remaining syrup. Pipe swirls of cream around the edge of the cake and fill the centre with the grated chocolate. Decorate with cherries.

Function	Cooking time	Preheating	Shelf position
Fan heat 160ºC	25 – 30 minutes	No	First

BAKED CHERRY CHEESECAKE

Preparation time:	Serves:	Total cooking time:
10 minutes + chilling	6 – 8	50 – 60 minutes

150g (5oz) unsalted butter

125g (4 1/2 oz) self-raising flour

110g (4 oz) caster sugar

3 eggs

450g (1lb) cream cheese

15ml (1 tbsp) cornflour

Few drops of vanilla essence

200g (7 oz) jar of pitted cherries

110g (4 oz) plain flour

Have ready an oblong cake tin 27.5 x 17.5 cm (11 x 7 inch) lined with silicone paper. To make the pastry, rub half the butter into the self-raising flour until it resembles fine breadcrumbs. Stir in 25g (1 oz) caster sugar. Whisk 2 eggs and gradually mix into the flour and butter until a firm dough is formed. Place in the refrigerator to chill for 30 minutes. Roll the pastry out on a floured surface, and use to line the prepared cake tin. Leave to rest in the refrigerator for a further 15 minutes. Mix together the cream cheese, cornflour, remaining egg, vanilla essence and 25g (1 oz) sugar. Spread over the pastry base. Drain the cherries and scatter over the cream cheese mixture. Rub the remaining butter into the plain flour until it resembles fine breadcrumbs, and stir in the remaining sugar. Spoon the crumble mixture over the cake. Bake in the oven until golden brown.

Function	Cooking time	Preheating	Shelf position
Fan heat 160ºC	50 – 60 minutes	No	First

ORANGE CREAM GENOESE SPONGE

Preparation time:	Serves:	Total cooking time:
10 minutes + chilling	8	35 minutes

40g (1½ oz) unsalted butter

75g (3 oz) plain flour

15ml (1 tbsp) cornflour

3 eggs

75g (3 oz) caster sugar

275ml (½ pint) double cream

150ml (¼ pint) soured cream

90ml (6 tbsp) orange curd

75g (3 oz) shredded coconut, toasted

Grease and base line 2 x 17.5cm (7 inch) sandwich tins. Melt the butter gently in a saucepan. Remove from the heat and leave to stand for a few minutes to allow any sediment to settle. Sift together the flour and cornflour. Place the eggs and sugar in a large bowl resting on a pan of hot water, and whisk until light and creamy. The mixture should be stiff enough to retain a trail when the whisk is lifted out. Remove from the heat and whisk until cool. Re-sift the flour and gently fold half into the egg mixture with a metal spoon. Make sure the butter is cooled until it just flows and, taking care not to let the sediment run in, pour the butter around the edges of the mixture. Gently fold the butter in with the remaining flour. Pour the mixture into the prepared tins. Bake until golden and springy to the touch. Turn out and cool on a wire rack.

To decorate, lightly whip the double cream until it just holds its shape. Carefully fold in the soured cream. Sandwich the sponges together with the orange curd and one third of the cream. Spread the remaining cream over the top and sides of the cake, and coat the sides with toasted coconut. Chill for 15 minutes before serving.

Function	Cooking time	Preheating	Shelf position
Fan heat 160°–170°C	25 – 30 minutes	Yes	First

BANANA TEABREAD

Preparation time:	Serves:	Total cooking time:
10 minutes	8	1hr – 1hr 15 mins

225g (8 oz) self-raising flour

2.5ml (½ tsp) salt

1.25ml (¼ tsp) ground nutmeg

110g (4 oz) unsalted butter

110g (4 oz) caster sugar and the grated rind of 1 lemon

2 large eggs, lightly beaten

105ml (7 tbsp) honey

450g (1 lb) ripe bananas, mashed

8 sugar lumps

Grease and base line a 1.2 litre (2 pint) loaf tin. Sift the flour, salt and nutmeg into a bowl. Rub in the butter until the mixture resembles fine breadcrumbs. Stir in the caster sugar, lemon rind, eggs, 90ml (6 tbsp) honey and mashed banana. Beat well until evenly mixed. Spoon the mixture into the prepared tin. Bake in the oven on the wire rack, until a skewer inserted into the centre of the teabread comes out clean. Leave to stand for 10 minutes before turning out. Gently warm the remaining honey and brush over the cooled teabread. Roughly crush the sugar lumps and scatter over the surface. Serve sliced, buttered if wished.

Function	Cooking time	Preheating	Shelf position
Conventional 180°C	1hr–1hr 15 mins	Yes	Second

MADEIRA CAKE

Preparation time:	Serves:	Total cooking time:
10 minutes	6 – 8	55 – 65 minutes

175g (6 oz) butter

175g (6 oz) caster sugar

3 eggs, beaten

30ml (2 tbsp) milk

5ml (1 tsp) vanilla essence

110g (4 oz) plain flour, sifted

110g (4 oz) self-raising flour, sifted

Grated rind of 1 lemon

Grease and base line a 17.5cm (7 inch) cake tin. Cream together the butter and sugar until pale and fluffy. Whisk in the beaten eggs, a little at a time. Add the milk and vanilla essence, then fold in the sifted flours and lemon rind. Turn the mixture into the tin and make a hollow in the cake with the back of a spoon. Bake in the oven until springy to the touch. To prevent over-browning, it might be necessary to cover the surface of the cake with brown paper towards the end of the cooking time. Leave to stand for 10 minutes, then turn out onto a wire rack and leave to cool before serving.

Function	Cooking time	Preheating	Shelf position
Fan heat 150ºC	55 – 65 minutes	No	First

CARROT CAKE

Preparation time:	Makes:	Total cooking time:
15 minutes	15 – 20 slices	40 – 50 minutes

175g (6 oz) soft brown sugar

200ml (7 fl oz) sunflower oil

2 eggs, lightly beaten

225g (8 oz) plain flour

5ml (1 tsp) bicarbonate of soda

5ml (1 tsp) cinnamon

2.5ml (½ tsp) mixed spice

Pinch of grated nutmeg

175g (6 oz) grated carrots

110g (4 oz) chopped walnuts

50g (2 oz) icing sugar, sifted

50g (2 oz) unsalted butter

110g (4 oz) full fat cream cheese

5ml (1 tsp) lemon juice

Place the sugar in a bowl, add the oil and beat together. Add the eggs and mix thoroughly. Sift the flour and bicarbonate of soda into the mixture and stir. Mix in the spices, carrots and 100g (3½ oz) of the walnuts. Pour into a 27.5 x 17.5cm (11 x 7 inch) greased tin lined with baking parchment. Bake in the oven on the wire rack, until a skewer inserted into the centre of the cake comes out clean. Allow to cool before icing. To make the topping, cream together the icing sugar and butter until light and fluffy. Beat in the cream cheese and lemon juice. Spread over the cake and decorate with the reserved walnuts. Cut into squares before serving.

Function	Cooking time	Preheating	Shelf position
Conventional 150ºC	40 – 50 minutes	Yes	Second

CARROT CAKE

ECCLES CAKES

ECCLES CAKES

Preparation time:	Makes:	Total cooking time:
10 minutes + resting	10 – 12	12 – 15 minutes

50g (2 oz) unsalted butter

110g (4 oz) soft brown sugar

50g (2 oz) finely chopped mixed peel

110g (4 oz) currants

5ml (1 tsp) cinnamon

350g (12 oz) puff pastry

Milk to glaze

Caster sugar to sprinkle

Have ready a baking tray, dampened with a little water. Melt the butter in a saucepan, and stir in the soft brown sugar, mixed peel, currants and cinnamon. Allow to cool. Roll out the pastry thinly, and cut 10 – 12 rounds using a 9cm (3½ inch) cutter. Place a teaspoonful of the filling mixture onto each pastry round. Draw up the pastry edges to enclose the filling, and seal with a little water. Turn each Eccles cake over and flatten a little, then place on the baking tray. Make 3 diagonal cuts in the top of each cake, and brush with milk. Leave to rest in the refrigerator for 10 minutes. Bake in the oven until golden. Sprinkle with caster sugar and then transfer to a wire rack to cool slightly before serving warm.

Function	Cooking time	Preheating	Shelf position
Fan heat 200ºC	12 – 15 minutes	Yes	Second

STICKY DATE & WALNUT CAKE

Preparation time:	Makes:	Total cooking time:
10 minutes + cooling	12 – 16 slices	1 hr 45 mins – 2 hours

110g (4 oz) raisins

225g (8 oz) chopped dates

175g (6 oz) sultanas

50g (2 oz) chopped walnuts

275g (10 oz) unsalted butter

400g (14 oz) tin condensed milk

275ml (10 fl oz) water

150g (5 oz) plain flour

150g (5 oz) wholewheat self-raising flour

Pinch of salt

2.5ml (½ tsp) bicarbonate of soda

50g (2 oz) glacé cherries, halved

15ml (1 tbsp) thick cut marmalade

Grease and base line a 20cm (8 inch) square cake tin. Place all the fruit, except the cherries, in a saucepan with the butter, condensed milk and water and bring to the boil, stirring well. Simmer for 3 minutes, stirring occasionally, then allow the mixture to cool. Meanwhile sieve all the dry ingredients into a bowl, tipping any remaining bran from the wholewheat flour into the bowl as well. Stir the glacé cherries, cooled fruit mixture and marmalade into the dry ingredients and mix well. Pour into the prepared tin and loosely cover with a double layer of greaseproof paper. Bake on the wire rack, then remove from the tin and cut into squares to serve.

Function	Cooking time	Preheating	Shelf position
Conventional 160ºC	1hr 45 mins – 2 hrs	Yes	Second

GINGERBREAD

Preparation time:	Serves:	Total cooking time:
5 minutes	8 – 10	1 hr – 1 hr 15 mins

450g (1 lb) plain flour

5ml (1 tsp) table salt

5ml (1 tsp) bicarbonate of soda

15ml (1 tbsp) baking powder

15ml (1 tbsp) ground ginger

150g (5 oz) unsalted butter

175g (6 oz) black treacle

200g (7 oz) soft brown sugar

175g (6 oz) golden syrup

275ml (½ pint) milk

1 egg, beaten

Grease and line a 23cm (9 inch) square cake tin. In a large bowl, sift together the flour, salt, bicarbonate of soda, baking powder and ginger. Place the butter, treacle, sugar and syrup into a saucepan and warm gently over a low heat until the mixture has melted. Remove from the heat, leave to cool slightly, then stir in the milk and beaten egg. Make a well in the centre of the dry ingredients, pour in the liquid and combine thoroughly. Pour the mixture into the prepared tin and bake on the wire rack until firm but springy to the touch. Remove from the oven and leave to stand for 10 minutes, then turn the cake out onto a wire rack and allow to cool.

Function	Cooking time	Preheating	Shelf position
Conventional 170°C	1 hr – 1 hr 15 mins	Yes	Second

FRESH LEMON CAKE

Preparation time:	Serves:	Total cooking time:
10 minutes	6 – 8	55 – 60 minutes

175g (6 oz) unsalted butter

175g (6 oz) caster sugar

3 eggs

175g (6 oz) self-raising flour, sifted

5ml (1 tsp) baking powder

Juice and finely grated rind of 1 lemon

110g (4 oz) icing sugar

In a large mixing bowl, cream the butter and sugar together. Gradually add the first egg and beat until light and fluffy. Add 15ml (1 tbsp) of the flour with each of the other two eggs, and beat until smooth. Fold in the rest of the flour, baking powder and lemon rind. Spoon the mixture into a lightly greased 900g (2 lb) loaf tin and bake in the oven until a skewer inserted into the centre of the cake comes out clean. Allow to cool. Sieve the icing sugar and mix with the lemon juice. Place the cake on a large piece of foil and pierce all over with a cocktail stick. Drizzle the icing over the cake, wrap in the foil and leave for 24 hours before slicing.

Function	Cooking time	Preheating	Shelf position
Fan heat 160°C	55 – 60 minutes	No	First

CHOCOLATE CARAMEL SHORTBREAD

Preparation time:	Makes:	Total cooking time:
10 minutes	30 slices	35 minutes

Base	275g (10 oz) plain flour
	25g (1 oz) cornflour and 30 – 45ml (2 – 3 tbsp) milk
	250g (9 oz) butter
	100g (3½ oz) caster sugar
Caramel	225g (8 oz) condensed milk
	225g (8 oz) unsalted butter
	225g (8 oz) light soft brown sugar
	60ml (4 tbsp) golden syrup and 2.5ml (½ tsp) vanilla essence
	300g (11 oz) plain chocolate

Sift the flour and cornflour into a bowl. Rub in the butter until the mixture resembles fine breadcrumbs. Mix in the sugar and knead lightly to form a dough, adding sufficient milk to bind. Press the mixture firmly and evenly onto a lightly greased baking tray, and pierce all over with a fork. Bake in the oven until lightly golden. Leave to cool. To make the caramel, put the condensed milk, butter, sugar, syrup and vanilla essence into a saucepan, and stir over a gentle heat until the sugar has dissolved. Bring to the boil and cook for 7 minutes, until a little of the mixture dropped into cold water forms a soft ball. Quickly spread the caramel over the shortbread. Melt the chocolate gently in a bowl over a pan of simmering water, and pour over the caramel. Leave until set, and cut into fingers with a sharp knife. Store in an airtight container.

Function	Cooking time	Preheating	Shelf position
Fan heat 160ºC	20 minutes	No	First

ORANGE & CHOCOLATE CHIP COOKIES

Preparation time:	Makes:	Total cooking time:
10 minutes + chilling	Approx. 24	15 – 20 minutes

75g (3 oz) unsalted butter
75g (3 oz) caster sugar
75g (3 oz) soft brown sugar
Grated rind of 1 orange
1 egg, lightly beaten
50g (2 oz) chocolate chips
175g (6 oz) self-raising flour

Place the butter, sugars and orange rind in a bowl, and cream together until light and smooth. Beat in the egg, and stir in the chocolate chips. Gently fold in the flour using a metal spoon, then leave to chill for 30 minutes. Divide the mixture into 24 walnut-sized balls and place well apart on 2 greased baking trays. Bake until light golden brown around the edges. Leave to cool on the trays for a few minutes before transferring to a cooling rack. Store in an airtight container.

Function	Cooking time	Preheating	Shelf position
Fan heat 160ºC	15 – 20 minutes	No	First and third

BOSTON FUDGE BROWNIES

Preparation time:	Makes:	Total cooking time:
10 minutes + cooling	20 squares	40 minutes

Fudge topping	200g (7 oz) caster sugar
	110g (4 oz) plain chocolate, grated
	275ml (½ pint) single cream
	110g (4 oz) butter, cut into pieces
	Few drops of vanilla essence
Brownies	250g (9 oz) butter, softened
	250g (9 oz) plain chocolate, grated
	250g (9 oz) soft dark brown sugar
	250g (9 oz) self-raising flour
	4 eggs, lightly beaten
	175g (6 oz) chopped hazelnuts
	60–90ml (4–6 tbsp) milk

For the fudge topping, place the sugar, grated chocolate and cream in a saucepan. Melt over a low heat and bring to the boil, stirring well, until the mixture thickens and a small amount dropped into cold water forms a soft ball. Remove from the heat, add the butter and vanilla essence, and stir until smooth. When the mixture has cooled a little, beat vigorously until it has thickened. Leave to cool completely. Meanwhile, lightly oil a baking tray. Melt the butter and chocolate in a bowl over a pan of simmering water. Stir in the sugar and leave to cool. Sift the flour into a large bowl, make a well in the centre, and pour in the chocolate mixture. Gradually mix together, bringing the flour into the chocolate mixture until well blended. Beat in the eggs and add the hazelnuts. Stir in enough milk to give a soft dropping consistency. Spoon the mixture into the prepared tray. Bake for about 25–30 minutes until a skewer inserted into the centre comes out clean. Leave to cool. Spread the topping over the cooled cake, and cut into squares.

Function	Cooking time	Preheating	Shelf position
Fan heat 160ºC	25 – 30 minutes	No	First

CHERRY GARLAND BISCUITS

Preparation time:	Makes:	Total cooking time:
10 minutes	Approx. 24 biscuits	20 – 25 minutes

225g (8 oz) butter, softened
50g (2 oz) icing sugar, sifted
200g (7 oz) plain flour
150g (5 oz) cornflour
Vanilla essence
12 glacé cherries, halved

Lightly grease 2 baking trays. Cream together the butter and icing sugar until pale and fluffy. Sift in the flours with a few drops of vanilla essence. Beat the mixture until very soft and smooth. Spoon into a piping bag with a 1cm (½ inch) star nozzle. Pipe swirls onto the trays, allowing room to spread. Press a cherry half onto the top of each. Bake until lightly golden. Cool for a minute, then slide onto a wire rack.

Function	Cooking time	Preheating	Shelf position
Fan heat 170ºC	20 –25 minutes	No	First and third

BOSTON FUDGE BROWNIES

SHREWSBURY BISCUITS

Preparation time:	Makes:	Total cooking time:
5 minutes + chilling	Approx. 24 biscuits	15 minutes

110g (4 oz) butter and 150g (5 oz) caster sugar

2 egg yolks, lightly beaten

225g (8 oz) plain flour and the finely grated rind of 1 lemon

Cream the butter and sugar together in a bowl until pale and fluffy. Gradually add the egg yolks to the creamed mixture, beating well after each addition. Stir in the flour and lemon rind and mix to a firm dough. Chill for 15 minutes. Roll out on a lightly floured surface to a thickness of 0.5cm (¼ inch). Using a 6.5cm (2½ inch) fluted cutter, cut into rounds and place on 2 greased baking trays. Bake until lightly golden and firm to the touch. Cool on a wire rack and store in an airtight container.

Function	Cooking time	Preheating	Shelf position
Fan heat 160°C	15 minutes	No	First and third

BRANDY SNAPS

Preparation time:	Makes:	Total cooking time:
10 minutes	12	10 – 12 minutes

50g (2 oz) unsalted butter

30ml (2 tbsp) golden syrup and 50g (2 oz) caster sugar

50g (2 oz) plain flour and 2.5ml (½ tsp) ground ginger

30ml (2 tbsp) brandy

Finely grated rind of half a lemon

150ml (¼ pint) double cream and 15ml (1 tbsp) icing sugar

Grease and line 2 baking trays. Melt the butter, syrup and sugar in a saucepan over a low heat until the sugar has dissolved. Remove from the heat. Sift the flour and ginger together. Stir into the butter mixture, together with 5ml (1 tsp) of the brandy and lemon rind. Using a teaspoon, drop spoonfuls of the mixture onto the baking trays, leaving a 10cm (4 inch) gap between each one and bake until bubbly and golden. Remove from the oven and allow to cool for 2 minutes, before loosening from the baking trays with a palette knife. Roll each one round the handle of a buttered wooden spoon. Leave for a few seconds to harden slightly, then twist off. Allow to cool, and store in an airtight container. To serve, whip the cream until stiff, then whisk in the rest of the brandy and the icing sugar. Spoon into a piping bag and pipe into either end of the snaps. NB: if the biscuits set before they have been rolled, soften by returning to the oven for a few seconds.

Function	Cooking time	Preheating	Shelf position
Fan heat 170°C	8 – 10 minutes	Yes	First and third

MERINGUES

Preparation time:	Makes:	Total cooking time:
5 minutes	12 – 16	3 – 4 hours

2 egg whites

110g (4 oz) caster sugar

Line an oven baking tray with silicone paper. Put the egg whites into a grease free bowl, and whisk until stiff. Gradually whisk in half the sugar, sprinkling in about 10ml (2 tsp) at a time. Lightly fold in the remaining sugar, using a metal spoon. Spoon into a piping bag fitted with a large nozzle, and pipe onto the prepared baking tray. Bake in the oven until the meringues are firm, crisp and dry. Leave to cool on a wire rack. Store in an airtight container. To serve, sandwich together with whipped cream and fresh fruit.

Function	Cooking time	Preheating	Shelf position
Fan heat 60 – 70°C	3 – 4 hours	No	First

LUXURY MINCE PIES

Preparation time:	Makes:	Total cooking time:
15 minutes + chilling	12	20 – 25 minutes

175g (6 oz) plain flour

Pinch of salt

75g (3 oz) butter

25g (1 oz) caster sugar

1 egg, beaten

350g (12 oz) luxury mincemeat (see page 138)

Milk to brush

Icing sugar to dust

Sift the flour and salt into a large bowl. Rub in the butter until the mixture resembles fine breadcrumbs, then mix in the sugar. Add the egg and a little water, if necessary, and mix to a fairly firm dough. Place in the refrigerator for 30 minutes. When chilled, roll out the pastry on a floured surface, then cut into 12 x 7.5cm (3 inch) circles and 12 x 6cm (2½ inch) circles. Line a greased patty tin with the larger circles, and put a teaspoonful of mincemeat into each one. Top with the smaller circles of pastry, sealing the edges with a little water, then brush the tops with milk. Slit the lids with a knife, then bake until the pies are golden brown. Cool on a wire rack and dust with icing sugar before serving.

Function	Cooking time	Preheating	Shelf position
Fan heat 190°C	20 – 25 minutes	No	First

BLUEBERRY MUFFINS

Preparation time:	Serves:	Total cooking time:
15 minutes	6	20 minutes

150g (5 oz) plain flour

7.5ml (½ tbsp) baking powder

1.25ml (¼ tsp) salt

1 egg, room temperature

50g (2 oz) vanilla sugar
(or caster sugar with a few drops of vanilla essence)

110ml (4 fl oz) tepid milk

50g (2oz) butter, melted and cooled

110g (4 oz) small blueberries

20g (¾ oz) sugar cubes, roughly crushed

Sift the flour, baking powder and salt into a bowl. In a separate bowl mix together the egg, sugar, milk and melted butter. Lightly re-sift the dry ingredients onto the egg mixture and stir lightly and quickly. It will have a rough, uneven appearance. Carefully fold the blueberries into the mixture with the minimum of agitation. Divide the mixture between 6 well greased muffin tins, and sprinkle with the crushed sugar cubes. Bake until well risen and golden brown. Allow to cool in the tins for 5 minutes before turning out. Serve warm with clotted cream.

Function	Cooking time	Preheating	Shelf position
Fan heat 200°C	20 minutes	No	First

SPICED SULTANA & ORANGE SCONES

Preparation time:	Makes:	Total cooking time:
10 minutes	16 – 18 scones	20 – 25 minutes

450g (1 lb) self-raising flour

5ml (1 tsp) salt

10ml (2 tsp) baking powder

125g (4½ oz) unsalted butter

Grated rind of 1 large orange

75g (3 oz) caster sugar

10ml (2 tsp) ground cinnamon

125g (4½ oz) sultanas

225ml (8 fl oz) milk

15ml (1 tbsp) orange juice

15ml (1 tbsp) golden syrup

Sift the flour, salt and baking powder into a large bowl. Rub in the butter until the mixture resembles fine breadcrumbs, then stir in the orange rind, sugar, cinnamon and sultanas. Add the milk and mix to a fairly firm dough. Roll out on a floured surface to a thickness of 2.5cm (1 inch) and cut into rounds with a 5cm (2 inch) cutter. Mix together the orange juice and the golden syrup, and brush liberally over the scones. Place on a lightly greased baking tray and bake until well risen and golden brown. Cool on a wire rack, before serving with orange curd and cream.

Function	Cooking time	Preheating	Shelf position
Fan heat 210ºC	20 –25 minutes	Yes	First or third

SAVOURY CHEESE & BACON SCONES

Preparation time:	Makes:	Total cooking time:
10 minutes	12	20 – 25 minutes

225g (8 oz) self-raising flour

Pinch of salt

5ml (1 tsp) baking powder

40g (1½ oz) butter

110g (4 oz) mature Cheddar, finely grated

5ml (1 tsp) mustard powder

2 rashers smoked bacon, chopped and lightly cooked

150ml (¼ pint) milk

Lightly grease a baking tray. Sift the flour, salt and baking powder together, and rub in the butter until the mixture resembles fine breadcrumbs. Stir in half the cheese, the mustard powder and bacon, and enough milk to give a fairly soft, light dough. Roll out on a floured surface to 2cm (¾ inch) thick and cut into rounds using a 5cm (2 inch) cutter. Place onto the baking tray, brush the tops with a little milk and sprinkle with the remaining cheese. Bake until well risen and golden brown.

Function	Cooking time	Preheating	Shelf position
Fan heat 210ºC	20 –25 minutes	Yes	First or third

ALL BUTTER LARDY CAKE

Preparation time:	Makes:	Total cooking time:
10 minutes + proving	9 slices	25 – 35 minutes

10g (½ oz) fresh yeast
or 10ml (2 tsp) dried yeast and 10ml (2 tsp) caster sugar

300ml (11 fl oz) tepid water

450g (1 lb) strong plain flour and 10ml (2 tsp) salt

15ml (1 tbsp) cooking oil

110g (4 oz) butter

75g (3 oz) caster sugar and 5ml (1 tsp) mixed spice

75g (3 oz) sultanas and 30ml (2 tbsp) icing sugar

Grease a tin measuring 22.5 x 22.5cm (9 x 9 inch). Blend the fresh yeast with the water. For dried yeast dissolve the sugar in the water, sprinkle the yeast over and leave in a warm place until frothy. Sift the flour and salt into a basin and stir in the yeast mixture. Add the oil to give a soft dough, then beat until smooth. Leave to rise in the fan oven set at 40°C until doubled in size. Turn the dough out onto a lightly floured surface and knead for 5–10 minutes until smooth and elastic. Roll out to an oblong strip 0.5cm (¼ inch) thick. Cover two-thirds of the dough with half of the butter, placing it on in small knobs. Mix the sugar, mixed spice and sultanas together and sprinkle half over the dough. Fold and roll out as for flaky pastry. Repeat the process with the remaining butter and sugar mixture. Fold and roll once more. Place the dough in the prepared tin, pressing it down so that it fills the corners. Cover and leave to rise in the fan oven at 40°C until doubled in size. Brush with oil and mark the top with a cross. Bake in the oven on the wire rack. Leave to cool, then dust with icing sugar.

Function	Cooking time	Preheating	Shelf position
Conventional 220°C	25 – 35 minutes	Yes	Second

HOT CROSS BUNS

Preparation time:	Makes:	Total cooking time:
10 minutes + proving	12	20 – 25 minutes

5ml (1 tsp) granulated sugar

275ml (½ pint) tepid milk

20ml (4 tsp) dried yeast

450g (1 lb) strong white flour

5ml (1 tsp) salt

5ml (1 tsp) ground mixed spice and 5ml (1 tsp) ground nutmeg

110g (4 oz) caster sugar

50g (2 oz) unsalted butter

50g (2 oz) currants and 50g (2 oz) mixed peel, chopped

Lightly grease and flour 2 baking trays. Stir the granulated sugar into the milk and whisk in the dried yeast, then leave in a warm place for about 10 minutes until frothy. Meanwhile, sift the flour, salt and spices into a bowl. Stir in 50g (2 oz) of the caster sugar and rub in the butter. Make a well in the centre of the flour and pour in the yeast mixture. Mix well and turn out onto a floured surface. Knead for 10 minutes until smooth. Place in a clean bowl, cover with a clean tea towel and leave to rise in the fan oven at 40°C until doubled in size. Work in the currants and peel, until evenly distributed. Divide the dough into 12 pieces and shape into buns. Place on the baking trays, marking the top of each with a cross. Re-cover with a clean tea towel and leave to rise in the fan oven at 40°C for a further 30 minutes. Bake until the buns are golden brown and firm to the touch. Dissolve the remaining sugar with 30ml (2 tbsp) of warm water. Brush the hot buns with the glaze and cool on a wire rack.

Function	Cooking time	Preheating	Shelf position
Fan heat 170°C	20 –25 minutes	No	First and third

SUN-DRIED TOMATO BREAD

Preparation time:	Serves:	Total cooking time:
5 minutes + proving	4	20 minutes

5ml (1 tsp) sugar

125ml (4½ fl oz) tepid water

15ml (1 level tsp) dried yeast

450g (1 lb) strong plain flour

5ml (1 tsp) salt

24 fresh basil leaves

50 – 75g (2 – 3 oz) sun-dried tomatoes,
drained and finely chopped

15ml (1 tsp) olive oil

Freshly ground black pepper

Blend the sugar and water together in a bowl, then whisk in the dried yeast. Place in the oven set on fan heat at 40°C for approximately 10 minutes or until frothy. Sift the flour and salt into a bowl, then gradually add the yeast liquid and bind together with a further 175 – 200ml (6 – 7 fl oz) tepid water. Draw the dough together then turn out onto a lightly floured surface and knead for about 10 minutes until smooth and elastic. Place on a lightly greased baking tray, cover with a damp tea towel and leave to prove on the fan heat setting at 40°C for approximately 1 hour, or until the dough has doubled in size. Tear 12 of the basil leaves into small pieces and push them evenly into the dough along with two-thirds of the sun-dried tomatoes. Press the remaining tomatoes and whole basil leaves onto the surface of the dough and season with a little black pepper. Divide the mixture into 4 pieces, replace on the tray, and drizzle with the olive oil. Leave to prove once more for 30 minutes on fan heat for the dough to rise.

Bake in the oven until the loaves are golden and sound hollow when tapped underneath. Serve warm with roasted tomato and red pepper soup (see page 8)

Function	Cooking time	Preheating	Shelf position
Fan heat 190°C	20 minutes	No	First

CHEESY HERB LOAF

Preparation time:	Makes:	Total cooking time:
10 minutes	8 slices	40 – 50 minutes

225g (8 oz) self-raising flour and 10ml (2 tsp) baking powder

5ml (1 tsp) mustard powder

15ml (1 tbsp) fresh parsley, chopped

5ml (1 tsp) chives, chopped

110g (4 oz) mature Cheddar cheese, grated

25g (1 oz) unsalted butter and 150ml (5 fl oz) water

1 egg, beaten and 25g (1 oz) Red Leicester cheese, grated

Grease and base line a 450g (1 lb) loaf tin. Sift the flour, baking powder and mustard powder into a bowl, then stir in the herbs and grated Cheddar. Melt the butter in a saucepan and add to the flour mixture, along with the water and beaten egg. Mix thoroughly, then spoon the mixture into the prepared tin. Bake for 15 minutes. Remove from the oven and sprinkle over the Red Leicester. Return to the oven and continue cooking for the remaining time until golden brown. Turn onto a wire rack and cool slightly. Serve warm, spread with butter.

Function	Cooking time	Preheating	Shelf position
Fan heat 170°C	40 – 50 minutes	No	First

BROWN SODA BREAD

Preparation time:	Serves:	Total cooking time:
10 minutes	4	25 – 30 minutes

225g (8 oz) strong plain white flour

225g (8 oz) strong plain wholemeal flour

5ml (1 tsp) salt

15ml (1 tbsp) bicarbonate of soda

15ml (1 tbsp) cream of tartar

150ml (5 fl oz) milk

150ml (5 fl oz) water

15ml (1 tbsp) golden syrup

5ml (1 tsp) vinegar

Lightly grease and flour an oven baking tray. Sift the flours, salt, bicarbonate of soda and cream of tartar into a bowl. Mix together the milk, water, syrup and vinegar. Make a well in the centre of the dry ingredients and pour in the liquid. Mix to a fairly stiff dough with the blade of a knife. Knead lightly and shape into a round loaf. Place on the prepared baking tray and score a deep cross in the top using a sharp knife. Bake at the higher temperature for 15 minutes, then reduce the temperature and cook for a further 10 – 15 minutes, until well risen and golden brown. Leave to cool on a wire rack.

Function	Cooking time	Preheating	Shelf position
Conv. 220º + 200ºC	25 – 30 minutes	Yes	Second

GRANARY BREAD

Preparation time:	Makes:	Total cooking time:
5 minutes + proving	2 loaves	30 – 35 minutes

700g (1^1/$_2$ lb) granary flour

10ml (2 tsp) salt

1 sachet easy blend dried yeast

25g (1 oz) butter

425ml (3/4 pint) hand-hot water

Beaten egg to glaze

Mix together the flour, salt and the yeast in a bowl. Cut the butter into small pieces and rub into the flour. Pour the water into the flour and mix together quickly to form a rough ball. Draw together, then turn out onto a lightly floured surface. Knead the dough for 5 – 8 minutes, until smooth, elastic and no longer sticky. Divide the dough in half and shape each piece into a ball. Place on a greased and floured baking sheet. Cut a deep cross in the top of each loaf, then cover with a damp cloth. Place in the oven on fan heat, set at 40°C, to prove for 45 minutes, or until the dough has doubled in size. Brush the loaves with beaten egg and bake on the wire rack until the loaves are golden and sound hollow when tapped underneath. Leave to cool on a wire rack.

Function	Cooking time	Preheating	Shelf position
Conventional 220ºC	30 – 35 minutes	Yes	Second or third

SWEET AND
SAVOURY SAUCES
& PRESERVES

PATISSERIE CREAM

Preparation time:	Makes:	Total cooking time:
5 minutes	Approx. 425 ml (³/₄ pint)	10 minutes

2 eggs and 50g (2 oz) caster sugar

30ml (2 tbsp) plain flour and 30ml (2 tbsp) cornflour

275ml (¹/₂ pint) milk

A few drops of vanilla essence
or 15ml (1 tbsp) Amaretto

Cream the eggs and sugar together until pale and thick. Sift in the flour and cornflour and beat into the mixture with a little of the milk until smooth. Heat the remaining milk until almost boiling, and pour slowly onto the egg mixture, stirring continuously. Transfer the custard to a clean saucepan and stir over a low heat until the mixture thickens. Add the vanilla essence or the Amaretto and cook for a further 2 minutes. Cover the surface of the custard with clingfilm and allow to cool. Store in the refrigerator for up to 3 days.

FROZEN MERINGUE CREAM

Preparation time:	Serves:	Total freezing time:
5 minutes	4	6 hours

275ml (¹/₂ pint) double cream

1 quantity homemade meringues (see page 128)

45ml (3 tbsp) Cointreau

Whip the double cream until it holds its shape. Roughly break up the meringues and fold into the cream with the Cointreau. Spoon into an 850ml (1½ pint) soufflé dish. Cover and freeze for at least 6 hours. Serve from the freezer with spiced plums (see page 109), or use as an alternative to cream. NB: use homemade meringues, as bought ones will soften.

RICH CHOCOLATE SAUCE

Preparation time:	Serves:	Total cooking time:
5 minutes	4	5 minutes

225g (8 oz) good quality plain chocolate

25g (1 oz) unsalted butter

75ml (3 fl oz) milk

75ml (3 fl oz) single cream

10ml (2 tsp) vanilla essence

15ml (1 tbsp) cherry brandy or Kirsch (optional)

Break the chocolate into a basin placed over a pan of simmering water, and allow the chocolate to melt. Beat the butter, milk, cream, vanilla essence and liqueur into the chocolate, and stir until smooth. Leave to cool, then pour over filled profiteroles or chocolate-based puddings and desserts.

COFFEE CREAM SAUCE

Preparation time:	Serves:
5 minutes	4

275ml (¹/₂ pint) double cream

20–30ml (1½–2 tbsp) coffee essence

10ml (2 level tsp) icing sugar, sifted

25g (1 oz) walnuts, finely chopped

15ml (1 tbsp) Tia Maria

Whip the cream to a thick pouring consistency. Mix in the coffee essence, sugar, walnuts and Tia Maria. Pour the sauce over filled profiteroles, or serve with apricot puddings in place of toffee nut sauce (see page 97).

FRESH LEMON CURD

Preparation time:	Makes:	Total cooking time:
10 minutes	Approx. 900g (2 lb)	30 minutes

Grated rind and juice of 4 lemons and 4 eggs, beaten

110g (4 oz) unsalted butter and 450g (1 lb) caster sugar

Place all the ingredients in a bowl standing in a pan of simmering water. Stir until the sugar has dissolved and continue heating. Stir frequently for about 20 minutes, or until the curd has thickened. Leave to cool slightly, then strain into small sterilized jars. Cover the surface with waxed discs and the jars with cellophane. Store in the refrigerator for up to 1 month.

RASPBERRY LIQUEUR CONSERVE

Preparation time:	Makes:	Total cooking time:
5 minutes	Approx. 900g (2 lb)	15 minutes

450g (1 lb) fresh, clean raspberries

10ml (2 tsp) lemon juice

450g (1 lb) granulated sugar

15ml (1 tbsp) Kirsch or brandy

Have ready 2 ovenproof dishes. Put the raspberries and lemon juice in one and the sugar in the other. Place both dishes in the preheated oven and cook on the wire rack for 15 minutes. Remove from the oven and tip the sugar over the raspberries. Stir for 3 minutes to dissolve the sugar. Leave to stand for 20 minutes. Repeat the stirring process three times, leaving to stand for 20 minutes after each stirring. Mix in the liqueur and pot in sterilized jars. Cover the surface of the conserve with a disc of waxed greaseproof paper and the jars with cellophane. Label and store in a cool, dark place. This natural, fruity conserve

has a soft set. It is delicious served with ice cream or as a filling in cakes. NB: choose clean, unblemished raspberries. Do not wash, as the added water will affect the set.

Function	Cooking time	Preheating	Shelf position
Conventional 180°C	15 minutes	Yes	Third

PEAR CHEESE

Preparation time:	Makes:	Total cooking time:
10 minutes	Approx 900g (2 lb)	1 hour 30 minutes

1.8kg (4 lb) pears

140ml (4½ fl oz) water

Granulated sugar

Wash the fruit and remove the stalks. Do not peel or core. Quarter the pears and simmer in the water until very soft. Remove from the heat and rub through a sieve into a clean saucepan. Simmer again until reduced by a third. Weigh the pulp, then take the same weight of sugar and warm it in the oven for 15 minutes. Stir the warmed sugar into the pulp until it has dissolved. Return the mixture to the heat, and boil gently until the mixture becomes glossy and is firm enough to retain a trail when a spoon is drawn through it. Remove from the heat and pot in small sterilized jars. Serve with a cheese board or cold meat platter.

Function	Cooking time	Preheating	Shelf position
Fan heat 180°C	15 minutes	No	First

FRESH LEMON CURD

ORANGE SLICES IN COINTREAU

Preparation time:	Makes:	Total cooking time:
10 minutes	Approx. 2.25litres (4 pints)	1 hour

350g (12 oz) granulated sugar

6 firm oranges, unblemished

1 cinnamon stick

5ml (1 tsp) cloves

150ml (5 fl oz) Cointreau

Heat the sugar in the oven for 10 minutes. Put 425ml (¾ pint) of water into a large saucepan. Tip in the warmed sugar and heat gently until the sugar has dissolved, then bring to the boil and boil fiercely for 1 minute. Meanwhile, scrub the oranges clean and cut into 5mm (¼ inch) slices. Place the orange slices in the syrup, along with the cinnamon stick. Top up with 350ml (12 fl oz) boiling water, ensuring that all the slices are immersed. Poach gently for 40 minutes until tender. Remove and discard the cinnamon stick. Leave the orange slices to cool for about 10 minutes before packing into sterilized, dry, airtight jars with the cloves. Stir the Cointreau into the reserved syrup and pour over the orange slices. Leave to mature for up to 1 month. Use to garnish roast pork with fruity stuffing (see page 63), sugar-glazed baked gammon (see page 63), or to accompany ice cream based desserts. NB: make sure all the equipment used is scrupulously clean and the jars are sterilized before filling.

Function	Cooking time	Preheating	Shelf position
Fan heat 180ºC	10 minutes	No	First

LUXURY MINCEMEAT

Preparation time:	Makes:	Total cooking time:
15 minutes + standing	Approx. 2.3kg (5 lb)	2 hours 30 minutes

450g (1 lb) apples, peeled, cored and sliced

350g (12 oz) raisins

225g (8 oz) sultanas

225g (8 oz) currants

225g (8 oz) shredded suet

225g (8 oz) mixed peel

350g (12 oz) muscovado sugar

110g (4 oz) glacé cherries, quartered

Grated rind and juice of 2 lemons

Grated rind and juice of 2 oranges

50g (2 oz) almonds, roughly chopped

20ml (4 tsp) ground mixed spice

5ml (1 tsp) ground cinnamon

90ml (6 tbsp) brandy

Combine all the ingredients except the brandy in a large mixing bowl. Cover with a clean cloth and leave to stand for 12 hours or preferably overnight. Cover the bowl with foil, and place in the oven for about 2 hours 30 minutes at 100ºC. Allow to cool and, when cold, stir in the brandy. Use as a filling for mince pies, or pack into clean, dry, sterilized jars, and store in the refrigerator.

Function	Cooking time	Preheating	Shelf position
Fan heat 100ºC	2hrs 30 mins	No	First

AUTUMN CHUTNEY

Preparation time:	Makes:	Total cooking time:
30 minutes	Approx. 1.4kg (3 lb)	1 hour 15 minutes

450g (1 lb) Bramley apples, peeled, cored and chopped

225g (8 oz) onion, chopped

700g (1½ lb) tomatoes, chopped

50g (2 oz) stoned dates, finely chopped

50g (2 oz) blanched almonds, chopped

110g (4 oz) demerara sugar

5ml (1 tsp) salt

225ml (8 fl oz) distilled malt vinegar

5ml (1 tsp) mustard seeds

2.5ml (½ tsp) cayenne pepper

Combine all the ingredients in a flameproof casserole dish. Bring to the boil on the hob, stirring occasionally. Transfer to the oven and cook, uncovered, for 1 hour, stirring from time to time, until it reaches a thick, spooning consistency. Spoon into sterilized jars and cover with vinegar-proof lids. Label and store in a cool, dry, dark place to mature for up to 3 months unopened. Once open, keep in the refrigerator and use within a month. NB: to sterilize the jars, wash in hot, soapy water and rinse thoroughly. Place in the fan oven for about 20 minutes at 140°C, then carefully fill the jars while still hot.

Function	Cooking time	Preheating	Shelf position
Fan heat 185°C	1 hour	No	First

SPICED APRICOT & RAISIN CHUTNEY

Preparation time:	Makes:	Total cooking time:
10 minutes	Approx. 900g (2 lb)	50 minutes

225g (8 oz) ready to eat dried apricots

350g (12 oz) onions, finely chopped

Juice and rind of 1 orange

1 clove garlic, skinned and crushed

225g (8 oz) granulated sugar

50g (2 oz) raisins

5ml (1 tsp) Dijon mustard

1.25ml (¼ tsp) ground mixed spice

1.25ml (¼ tsp) ground cinnamon

5ml (1 tsp) salt

425ml (¾ pint) white wine vinegar

Chop the apricots into quarters. Put all the ingredients in a large heatproof bowl. Place in the oven and cook uncovered for 50 minutes, stirring occasionally, until the chutney has thickened and no excess liquid remains. Pour the chutney into warmed, sterilized jars and cover with airtight, vinegar-proof tops. Label and store in a cool, dry, dark place for 2–3 months to mature before eating. Once open, keep in the refrigerator and use within a month. NB: to sterilize the jars, wash in hot, soapy water and rinse thoroughly. Place in the fan oven for about 20 minutes at 140°C, then carefully fill the jars while still hot.

Function	Cooking time	Preheating	Shelf position
Fan heat 200°C	50 minutes	No	First

STROGANOFF SAUCE

Preparation time:	Serves:	Total cooking time:
5 minutes	4	20 minutes

50g (2 oz) butter and 1 large onion, chopped

225g (8 oz) mushrooms, sliced

Salt and freshly ground black pepper

150ml (¼ pint) white wine

250g (9 oz) crème fraîche

Grated nutmeg to garnish

Melt the butter in a saucepan. Add the onion and fry gently for a few minutes until softened. Add the mushrooms and continue cooking for a further 5 minutes. Season and stir in the wine and crème fraîche. Bring to the boil and allow the sauce to reduce and thicken, stirring continuously. Serve with cheese and nut roast (see page 84) or with fillet steaks as an alternative to Dijonnaise sauce (see page 61). Sprinkle with nutmeg just before serving.

TOMATO COULIS

Preparation time:	Serves:	Total cooking time:
5 minutes + standing	4	10 minutes

30ml (2 tbsp) olive oil

1 clove garlic, finely chopped

2 shallots, finely chopped

350ml (12 fl oz) passata sauce

Salt and freshly ground black pepper

4–5 fresh basil leaves

Heat the olive oil in a saucepan, and sweat the garlic and shallots until soft but not coloured. Stir in the passata sauce and heat slowly to just simmering point. Blend in a food processor until smooth. Season with salt and pepper. Tear the basil leaves to shreds and stir into the sauce just before serving. Serve warm with fish, vegetarian or meat dishes, or cold with salads. Tomato coulis can also be used on the base of pizzas or stir 30–45ml (2–3 tbsp) into cooked green beans before serving.

TOMATO SALSA

Preparation time:	Serves:
10 minutes + standing	4

8 firm, ripe tomatoes, skinned, seeded and diced

1 spring onion, chopped

1 clove garlic, finely chopped

15ml (1 tbsp) fresh coriander, chopped

15ml (1 tbsp) white wine vinegar

45ml (3 tbsp) olive oil

A few drops of hot chilli sauce

Salt and freshly ground black pepper

Mix the tomatoes, onion, garlic and the fresh coriander together in a bowl. Blend the vinegar, olive oil, chilli sauce and seasoning together and stir into the tomato mixture. Leave to stand for 15 minutes before serving as an accompaniment to salads, steaks, fish and curried dishes.

AROMATIC OILS

ALL PHOTOGRAPHS SUPPLIED BY ANTHONY BLAKE PHOTO LIBRARY: PHOTOGRAPHER AS INDICATED BELOW

Joy Skipper: Cover. Tim Imrie: Page 6. Milk Marque: Pages 9. 31. 55. 79. 85. 93. 110. 113. 121. 137. Gerrit Buntrock: Pages 15. 56. 77. 80. Merehurst Ltd: Page 20. 65. 70. 74. 89. Kieran Scott: Page 21. Phototheque Culinaire: Page 22. Simon Smith: Page 24. Andrew Sydenham: Pages 27. 114. 127. Anthony Blake: Pages 28. 33. 39. 43. 50. 64. 96. 101. 103. 106. Alain Proust: Page 36. Victor Watts: Page 45. James Murphy: Page 48. Tim Hill: Pages 59. 134. Stockfood: Page 90. Charlie Stebbings: Page 105. Neville Kuypers: Page 117. Heather Brown: Page 122 Rosenfeld Images Ltd: Page 141.